I0105714

God Searches the Heart

What's Hidden in Yours?

Dr. Phyllis Glass

KP PUBLISHING COMPANY

Copyright 2023 by Dr. Phyllis Glass

God Searches the Heart: What's Hidden in Yours?

All rights reserved. In accordance with the U.S. Copyright Act of 1976, the scanning, uploading, and electronic sharing of any part of this book without the permission of the publisher is unlawful piracy and theft of the author's intellectual property. If you would like to use material from this book (other than for review purposes), prior written permission must be obtained by contacting the publisher at info@kp-pub.com.

Thank you for your support of the author's rights.

ISBN: 978-1-960002-00-9 (Paperback)
ISBN: 978-1-960001-01-6 (eBook)
Library of Congress Control Number: Pending

Editor: Frank Williams
Cover Design: Juan Roberts, Creative Lunacy
Interior Design: Jennifer Houle
Literary Director: Sandra Slayton James

All Bible verses are taken from the King James Version unless otherwise noted.

DISCLAIMER: The author is not a medical professional; however, to be more descriptive in comparisons, some medical references have been used to highlight some heart conditions.

Published by:

Published by:
KP Publishing Company
Publisher of Fiction, Nonfiction & Children's Books
www.kp-pub.com

Printed in the United States of America

The condition of your hearts may affect your health and happiness.

Keep thy heart with all diligence; for out of it are the issues of life.

Proverbs 4:23

Contents

Foreword

IN DAILY LIFE, there are so many distractions. In fact, current research indicates that our average attention span has slowly declined from twelve seconds in 2000 to now eight seconds in the past few years. It means our focus is moving from one outward stimulus to the next. We are multi-tasking our remote work with home responsibilities. We are getting notified when our next work meeting is coming up and when our microwave popcorn is ready. With us looking outward so often, do we spend enough time looking inward? When we do look inward, are we able to ascertain if we are really doing well? Our bodies give us signs regularly of the condition of our spiritual hearts. Our emotions can often lead us to truths about the real state of our hearts. Because our heart is our true self, it is important that we take a good look at how we are doing from the inside out. Unfortunately, we often do not want to be still long enough to examine our hearts. I think this is why *God Searches the Heart—What's Hidden in Yours?* written by Dr. Phyllis Glass, is a must-read and fundamental to your transformational journey. Dr. Glass reveals the characteristics of our heart's physical and spiritual makeup. She also identifies the importance of our thoughts and how they can positively or negatively impact our heart condition and, ultimately, our general physical health. My desire is the same as the songwriter David, where he says in Psalm 51:10 (NIV), *"Create in me a pure heart, O God, and renew a steadfast spirit within me."* If this is your desire, too, this gem written by Dr. Glass will lead the way.

Pastor Michele Alanis
Executive Pastor
Living Praise Christian Church
North Hollywood and Palmdale, California

Introduction

MY MOTIVATION TO write this book was born out of my need to understand the significance of how important the condition of the human heart affects us. The intent is to emphasize the biblical aspects that provide many accuracies on how we are, act, or react to life based on the condition(s) of the human heart. Scripture reveals that many things are hidden in our hearts, which we are not often fully aware of.

Those things hidden in our hearts can positively or negatively affect the condition of our hearts in both a physical and spiritual sense. In addition, those conditions can and do play a significant role in our overall health and happiness. These conditions can also determine the advantages and benefits available because of God's promises when our hearts reflect our obedience to God's Word. These conditions also may determine the disadvantages and risks we might encounter when we are disobedient or reject God's statutes or commandments.

The contents of this book will cover the positive and negative impacts from both the physical and spiritual points of view. My focus is to tap into hearts regardless of whether they are Christian and to have them re-think its importance. Further, to understand the significance of how their heart condition is directly related to their overall health and happiness.

It is especially important to understand that to have a "change of heart" according to the Word of God will become one of the greatest benefits and rewards. We are commanded and encouraged to "guard" our hearts, our minds, our whole being if we want to be healthy and prosperous. The attention we give to these commands reflect how obedient we are to the word of God.

According to Bible verses that support the subject matter, readers will find more than fifty conditions of the heart and the positive or negative impact those conditions may have on your relationship with God. The characteristics of whether the condition represents either a "good" or "bad" heart are to show both the positive and negative impact that may be present.

The information contained within will provide valuable information that will affect and perhaps even cause a "change of heart" for the reader as you are encouraged and enlightened by the wealth of knowledge contained herein. When we know better, we do better.

PART I

CHAPTER 1

The Heart of Man

What happens when your heart is in a positive versus a negative state?

A. Physical Purpose/Condition According to Man:

The overall purpose and condition of our hearts according to man is to ensure that it functions in a manner that enables our bodies to perform daily in all the areas that are necessary to be sure all body parts are working properly.

What do Doctors and the Medical Community say about the Heart?

Dr. Greg E. Viehman, a physician that specializes in General Dermatology, writes on "Cardiology: The Spiritual Heart"[1] that speaks on the anatomy and physiology of the heart. Although he specializes in dermatology, he completed an internship in Internal Medicine. He also completed his master's degree in theology and is the author of two Christian books.

Dr. Viehman's testimony is that despite his professional success, and achievements, in his words, he "had a severe heart problem." This

---

1 Dr. Greg E. Viehman, MD

problem did not exist in his physical heart but in his spiritual heart. He further writes that he needed a "spiritual heart transplant, and that the Great Physician Jesus Christ, our Lord and Savior would be that one to perform the transplant."

His description of the heart is as most of us already know, that it is the most important organ in the body. He goes on to say, "It is the central pump and powerhouse that circulates the blood and provides oxygen and energy to all the cells. The article mention these statistics:

1. The heart beats about 100,000 times per day.
2. It will pump approximately 2,000 gallons of blood.
3. It will beat more than 2.5 billion times during an average lifetime."

He states, "Cardiology is the branch of medicine that deals with diseases and abnormalities of a human heart. The Bible mentions the heart 987 times, and almost all of these refer to our spiritual heart. We can assume that this is an essential topic for God. According to Matthew 22:37-38, the great commandment is to love God with all our hearts. It makes spiritual cardiology very important in our lives. One of the most important things in all scripture is to have a healthy heart. But what exactly is our spiritual heart? Before we can study the heart and heart disease, we need to understand the structure and function of our spiritual hearts. It will enable us to properly listen to our hearts and diagnose any problems so that God can provide healing and spiritual medicine."

Dr. Viehman says, "If you study the word for heart in the Old and New Testament it is actually quite complicated and complex. There are many different functions associated with the heart and there is overlap with other terms like spirit, mind, and soul. Overall, the heart is the seat or core aspect of our inner nature that makes up the real person that we are before God. According to Proverbs 4:3, it is called the wellspring of life."

To help us understand the heart and how it works, we will use an analogy and diagram as in, the heart is like a corporation that has inputs and outputs. Things come into the company and the company produces things as a result. The internal structure of the corporation consists of different departments under a CEO and set of company policies and rules.

His article references the biblical components of the heart according to the scripture referenced:

- Our **feelings and emotions**:
  For from within, out of the heart of men, proceed evil thoughts, adulteries, fornications, murders, thefts, covetousness, wickedness, deceit, lasciviousness, an evil eye, blasphemy, pride, foolishness: All of these evil things come from within, and defile the man.

  MARK 7:21-23

  Let not your heart be troubled, ye believe in God, believe also in me.

  JOHN 14:1

- Our **desires, motivations, and passions** can be found in (*Mark 7:21*) as outlined above.
- Our **thoughts imaginations, motives, and intentions**:
  And behold, certain of the scribes said within themselves. This man blasphemeth. And Jesus knowing their thoughts said, Wherefore think ye evil in your heart.

  MATTHEWS 9:3-4

3

- Our **reasoning and perception** can be found in:
  But there were certain of the scribes sitting there, and reasoning in their hearts. Why doth this man thus speak blasphemies? Who can forgive sins but God only? And immediately when Jesus perceived in his spirit that they so reasoned within themselves, he said unto them. Why reason ye things in your hearts?

  MARK 2:6-8

  And as the people were in expectation, and all men mused in their hearts of John, whether he were the Christ or not;

  LUKE 3:15

- Our **attitude and character** can be found in:
  Servants, obey in all things your masters according to the flesh; not with eyeservice, as menpleasers; but in singleness of heart, fearing God: And whatsoever ye do, do it heartily as to the Lord, and not unto men:

  COLOSSIANS 3:22-23

- Our **will** can be found in:
  Not with eyeservice, as menpleasers; but as the servants of Christ, doing the will of God from the heart;

  EPHESIANS 6:6

- **The law of God is written there according to:**
  For as many as have sinned without law shall also perish without law: and as many as have sinned in the law shall be judged by the law; For not the hearers of the law are just before God, but the doers of the law shall be justified. For

4

when the Gentiles, which have not the law, do by nature the things contained in the law, these, having not the law, are a law unto themselves: Which shew the work of the law written in their hearts, their conscience also bearing witness, and their thoughts the mean while accusing or else excusing one another. In the day when God shall judge the secrets of men by Jesus Christ according to my gospel.

ROMANS 2:12-16

- **The Holy Spirit is available if a person is saved according to:**
  And hope maketh not ashamed; because the love of God is shed abroad in our hearts by the Holy Ghost which is given unto us.

ROMANS 5:5

Now he which stablisheth us with you in Christ, and hath anointed us, is God; Who hath also sealed us, and given the earnest of the Spirit in our hearts.

2 CORINTHIANS 1:21-22

- **The knowledge of God and the desire for God according to:**
  He hath made every thing beautiful in his time: also he hath set the world in their heart, so that no man can find out the work that God maketh from the beginning to the end.

ECCLESIASTICS 3:11

Because that which may be known of God is manifest in them; for God hath shewed it unto them. For the invisible things of him from the creation of the world are clearly seen, being understood by the things that are made even his eternal power and Godhead; so that they are without excuse: Because that, when they knew God, they glorified him not as God, neither were thankful; but became vain in their imaginations, and their foolish heart was darkened.

ROMANS 1:19-21

If we look at the physiology and functions of the heart, we know that the heart is complex and responsible for everything that we do and feel and say according to Mark 7:21-23. In addition, it is also functions in the following areas:

- **Location of saving faith** according to:
  But what saith it? The word is nigh thee, even in thy mouth, and in thy heart: that is, the word of faith, which we preach.

  ROMANS 10:8

- The **conviction of sin and repentance**:
  Now when they heard this, they were pricked in their heart, and said unto Peter and to the rest of the apostles, Men and brethren, what shall we do? Then Peter said unto them, Repent, and be baptized every one of you in the name of Jesus Christ for the remissions of sins, and ye shall receive the gift of the Holy Ghost.

  ACTS 2:37-38

My little children, let us not love in word, neither in tongue; but in deed and in truth. And hereby we know that we are of the truth, and shall assure our hearts before him. For if our heart condemn us, God is greater than our heart, and knoweth all things. Beloved, if our heart condemn us not, then have we confidence toward God.

1 JOHN 3:18-21

- **Spiritual hearing** and **spiritual vision** according to:
  And in them is fulfilled the prophecy of Esaias, which saith,. By hearing ye shall hear, and shall not understand and seeing ye shall see, and shall not perceive. For this people's heart is waxed gross, and their ears are full of hearing, and their eyes they have closed; lest at any time they should see with their eyes and hear with their ears, and should understand with their heart, and should be converted, and I should heal them. But blessed are your eyes, for they see; and your ears, for they hear.

MATTHEW 13:14-15

- The word of God is **received in the heart**:
  When any one heareth the word of the kingdom, and understandeth it not, then cometh the wicked one, and catcheth away that which was sown in his heart. This is he which received seed by the way side.

MATTHEWS 13:19

- The **origin of our words**:
  O generation of vipers, how can ye, being evil, speak good things? for out of the abundance of the heart the mouth speaketh. A good man out of the good treasure of the heart bringeth forth good things: and an evil man out of the evil treasure bringeth forth evil things. But I say unto you, That

every idle word that men shall speak, they shall give account thereof in the day of judgment. For by thy words thou shalt be justified, and by thy words thou shall be condemned.

MATTHEWS 12:34-37

B. Spiritual Purpose/Condition According to God

God Searches the Heart

The heart is the locus of physical and spiritual being and represents the central wisdom of feeling as opposed to the head-wisdom of reason. It is compassion and understanding, life-giving and complex. It is a symbol for love.

The heart is deceitful above all things, and desperately wicked: who can know it? I the Lord search the heart, I try the reins, even to give every man according to his ways, and according to the fruit of his doings.

JEREMIAH 17;9-10

But as it is written, Eye hath not seen, nor ear heard, nether have entered into the heart of man, the things which God hath prepared for them that love him. But God hath revealed them unto us by his Spirit: for the Spirit searcheth all things, yea, the deep things of God.

1 CORINTHIANS 2:9-10

But the Lord said unto Samuel, Look not on his countenance, or on the height of his stature; because I have refused him: for the Lord seeth not as man seeth; for man looketh on the outward appearance, but the Lord looketh on the heart.

1 SAMUEL 16:7

d he that searcheth the hearts knoweth what is the mind of the Spirit, because he maketh intercession for the saints according to the will of God.

ROMANS 8:27

We are commanded to guard our hearts

Be careful for nothing; but in every thing by prayer and supplication with thanksgiving let your requests be made known unto God. And the peace of God, which passeth all understanding, shall keep your hearts and minds through Christ Jesus.

PHILIPPIANS 4:6-7

My flesh and my heart may faileth, but God is the strength of my heart, and my portion forever.

PSALM 73:26

My son, forget not my law; but let thine heart keep my commandments. For length of days, and long life, and peace, shall they add to thee. Let not mercy and truth forsake thee: bind them about thy neck; write them upon the table of thine heart: So shalt thou find favour and good understanding in the sight of God and man. Trust in the Lord, with all thine heart; and lean not unto thine own understanding. In all thy ways acknowledge him, and he shall direct thy paths.

PROVERBS 3:1-6

Peace I leave with you, my peace I give unto you; not as the world giveth, give I unto you. Let not your heart be troubled, neither let it be afraid.

JOHN 14:27

We have to be serious about those areas where God has commanded us to perform and practice a specific behavior. Guarding our hearts and our minds are among those. Scripture provides us with instructions on how and why we should endeavor to accomplish this.

Here are three ways we can put forth the effort and demonstrate through practice that we are sincere about keeping our hearts and minds guarded:

1. We can look to God to guard our hearts and minds

Because God knows the heart of man, He expects us to stay in a constant state of walking in a manner that will enable us to be worthy of receiving the rewards He has in store for us. Only God can cleanse our hearts and minds from the sinful nature that pursues us, but He needs our cooperation to exercise good judgment and discipline.

> *The heart is deceitful above all things, and desperately wicked: who can know it? If the Lord search the heart, I try the reins, even to give every man according to his ways, and according to the fruit of his doings.*
>
> JEREMIAH 17:9-10

We have an obligation to examine ourselves and go to God and ask Him to search our hearts and our minds.

> *Search me, O God, and know my heart: try me, and know my thoughts:*
> *And see if there be any wicked way in me, and lead me in the way everlasting.*
>
> PSALM 139:23-24

This scripture outlines six requests David made to God:
1. Search me.
2. Know my heart.
3. Try me.
4. Know my thoughts.
5. See if there is any wicked way in me.
6. Lead me in the way everlasting.

2. **We can offer prayer and moral principles to guard our hearts and minds**

   Finally brethren, whatsoever things are <u>true</u>, whatsoever things are <u>honest</u>, whatsoever things are <u>just</u>, whatsoever things are <u>pure</u>, whatsoever things are <u>lovely</u>, whatsoever things are of good <u>report</u>; if there be any virtue, and if there be any praise, think on these things.

   PHILIPPIANS 4:8

There are six things that we should meditate on:
1. True things or all that is in harmony with eternal creation.
2. Honest things – all that is decent, honorable and reflect Christian principles.
3. Just things – all that is harmony with justice and righteousness.
4. Pure things – all that is chaste and holy for the body and the soul.
5. Lovely things – those things that are pleasing and tends to bless others.
6. Things of good report – all that is in harmony with good and are praiseworthy.

Keep thy <u>heart</u> with all diligence; for out of it are the issues of life. Put away from thee a froward <u>mouth</u>, and perverse lips put far from thee. Let thine <u>eyes</u> look right on, and let thine <u>eyelids</u> look straight before thee. Ponder the path of thy <u>feet</u>, and let all thy ways be established. Turn not to the right <u>hand</u> nor to the left: remove thy <u>foot</u> from evil.

PROVERBS 4:23-27

In these scriptures, we are commanded to guard many of our bodily parts and keep them under control as follows:

- To guard the heart keeps us from going astray, because out of it are the issues of life.
- To guard the mouth prevents froward or evil speech, and governs what we say.
- To guard the eyes prevents us from setting our sights on things of a sinful nature.
- To guard our feet will allow us to walk in a righteous path and lead us away from evil.
- To guard our hands keeps us in doing good and not engaged in idle or mischievous works.

Examine yourself:

Examine yourselves, whether ye be in the faith; prove your own selves. Know ye not your own selves, how that Jesus Christ is in you, except ye be reprobates? But I trust that ye shall know that we ae not reprobates.

2 CORINTHIANS 13:5-6

But those things which proceed out of the mouth come forth from the heart; and they defile the man. For out of the heart proceed evil thoughts, murder, adulteries, fornication, thefts, false witness, blasphemies: These are the things which defile a man: but to eat with unwashed hands defileth not a man.

MATTHEW 15:18-20

We should endeavor to constantly examine ourselves to ensure our walk coincides with our talk. The fruit we bear should demonstrate that our maturity and growth correlate directly with our beliefs and principles in the word of God. Our integrity and moral compass should reflect that belief as being good, true, and profitable for our daily living.

The condition of our hearts is somewhat defined by both our mental and physical health. That condition is often determined by how we allow positive or negative thoughts and emotions to affect our daily existence. An article by Kristina Robb-Dover on "How Negative Emotions Affect Health."[2]

She states that first, we must understand and define negative emotions as follows:

"While there have been significant disputes among experts over exactly how many basic emotions exists, researchers claim in a study published in *Current Biology* that there are four:

- Happiness
- Sadness
- Fear/surprise
- Anger/disgust

---

2 Kristina Robb-Davis, How Negative Emotions Affect Health, June 12, 2020

According to the *APA Dictionary of Psychology*, emotions consist of behaviors we have in response to an external event, our subjective experience of that event and our bodies' automatic physiological response to that event.

She goes on to outline:

How Can Stress Negatively Affect Your Mental Health?

"According to the National Institute of Mental Health, when stress is ongoing, its effects can differ greatly from short-term, acute stress that occurs in an isolated incident. Chronic stress not only keeps the body from discerning when it's safe to turn off its physiological responses, but it can keep the mind hooked on certain emotions past their point of welcome.

When chronic stress brings on long-lasting sadness, anger or fear, these emotions can affect our mental health by inducing depression, irritability, anxiety, and substance abuse.

These negative emotions in chronic form can become disorders that:

- Create and encourage a cycle of negative thought patterns
- Can lead a person to isolate, spurring more pervasive feelings of insecurity, low self-esteem and loneliness."

Can Negative Emotions Affect Your Physical Health?

Along with our mental health, persistent or overwhelming negative emotions can greatly affect our physical health. Chronic or heightened levels of stress cause our bodies to persistently release the same hormones used to induce our fight, freeze, or flight reflexes.

Some of the physiological response that can save your life include decreased appetite, slowing down of bodily functions, sweating, decreased need for sleep and a faster or slower heart rate, increased adrenaline and increased sensitivity to stimuli can also lead to anxiety, feelings of being overwhelmed and irritability.

The National Institute of Mental Health states "that persistent, chronic levels of stress and negative emotions can contribute to:

- High blood pressure
- Compromised immune system
- Heart disease
- Diabetes
- Dehydration
- Digestive issues
- Insomnia

Additionally, stress can lead to muscle tension and aches, cause malnutrition from a decreased appetite and make it more difficult for your body to grow and heal from injuries. Not only are these conditions bad for your health, but they can greatly affect your quality of life."

CHAPTER 2

Characteristics of a Good and Positive Heart

PART 1 OF this book outline those characteristics that best describe those who possess the positive attributes displayed and/or demonstrated by followers of Christ, and those whose lives reflect their obedience to the word of God. The condition of their heart is key to their being able to maintain a righteous attitude before God.

How positive thinking and/or thoughts and emotions can affect your heart and your health.

> *Casting down imaginations, and every high thing that exalteth itself against the knowledge of God, and bringing into captivity every thought to the obedience of Christ:*
>
> 2 CORINTHIANS 10:5

Advantages of positive thinking: Assistance, gift, relief, privilege, fringe benefit, bonus.

*Studies show that there is plenty of documentation that having a positive or optimistic view of life can also produce positive results in our health as well as our overall daily living. These studies also outline that people who tend to display positive emotions are less likely to experience the stressors that cause a higher heart rate or high blood pressure.

People in this group who must confront stress, are more apt to lean toward healthy methods for handling those challenges by choosing positive plans of action by applying problem-solving, stress management or techniques, meditation, and prayer.

When people are free to express their feelings or emotions without being judged or criticized are less likely to have their health impacted by stress. However, when emotions or feelings are suppressed, especially if they have had a negative experience or encounter, it can affect the body in a negative way which can ultimately lead to health problems.

We should never underestimate the power of forgiveness. Forgiveness can result in being in a more positive mental, emotional, and physically healthy state. Medical science shows by releasing others from their transgressions against us, can cause a sense of relief and lower our blood pressure, which in turn improves our cardiovascular health.

Benefits, Rewards and Advantages:
Six Benefits of Knowing God:
- First, to know God is to have protection.
- Second, to know God is to have provision.
- Third, to know God is to be drawn to those who are righteous.
- Fourth, to know God is to be troubled by sin.
- Fifth, to know God is to be joyfully content.
- Sixth, to know God is to be faithfully guided.

Twenty Benefits of the Word of God (The Bible)
(1) It is the source of <u>faith</u>:
So, then faith cometh by hearing, and hearing by the word of God.

ROMANS 10:17

(2) It is the source of <u>salvation</u>:
And that from a child thou hast known the holy scriptures, which are able to make thee wise unto salvation through faith which is in Christ Jesus.

2 TIMOTHY 3:15

For I am not ashamed of the gospel of Christ;, for it is the power of God unto salvation to every one that believeth; to the Jew first, and also to the Greek.

ROMANS 1:16

Being born again, not of corruptible seed, but of incorruptible, by the word of God, which liveth and abideth for ever.

1PETER 1:23

Wherefore lay apart all filthiness and superfluity of naughtiness, and receive with meekness the engrafted word, which is able to save your souls.

JAMES 1:21

(3) It is the source of <u>truth</u>:
Sanctify them through thy truth: they word is truth.

JOHN 17:17

(4) It is the source of <u>freedom</u>:

Then said Jesus to those Jews which believed on him, if ye continue in my word, then are ye my disciples indeed; And ye shall know the truth, and the truth shall make you free.

JOHN 8:31-32

(5) It is the source of <u>freedom from error</u>:

Jesus answered and said unto them, Ye do err, not knowing the scriptures, nor the power of God.

MATTHEW 22:29

(6) It is the source of <u>spiritual food</u>:

But he answered and said, It is written, Man shall not live by bread alone, but by every word that proceedeth out of the mouth of God.

MATTHEW 4:4

It is the spirit that quickeneth; the flesh profiteth nothing; the words that I speak unto you, they are spirit, and they are life.

JOHN 6:63

(7) It is the source of <u>growth</u>:

As newborn babies, desire the sincere milk of the word, that ye may grow thereby.

1 PETER 2:2

For this cause also thank we God without ceasing, because when ye received the word of God which ye heard of us, ye received it not as the word of men, but as it is in truth, the

word of God which effectually worketh also in you that
believe.

1 THESSALONIANS 2:13

(8) It is the source of <u>victory over temptation</u>:
*Thy word have I hid in mine heart, that I might not sin
against thee.*

PSALM 119:11

(9) It is the source of <u>happiness or blessedness</u>:
*Blessed is the man that heareth me, watching daily at my
gates, waiting at the posts of my doors.*

PROVERBS 8:34

*But he said, Yea rather, blessed are they that hear the word of
God, and keep it.*

LUKE 11:28

(10) It is the source of <u>purity (Holiness)</u>:
*Wherewithal shall a young man cleanse his way? by taking
heed thereto according to thy word.*

PSALM 119:9

ctify them through thy truth: thy word is truth.

JOHN 17:17

(11) It is the Source of <u>self-diagnosis (Spiritual check-up)</u>:
*For the word of God is quick, and powerful, and sharper than
any twoedged sword, piercing even to the dividing asunder of*

soul and spirit, and of the joints and marrow, and is a discerner of the thoughts and intents of the heart.

HEBREWS 4:12

(12) It is the source of <u>guidance</u>:

Thy word is a lamp unto my feet, and a light unto my path.

PSALM 119:105

(13) It is the source of <u>comfort</u>:

For whatsoever things were written aforetime were written for our learning, that we through patience and comfort of the scriptures might have hope.

ROMANS 15:4

(14) It is the source for <u>answered prayer</u>:

If ye abide in me, and my words abide in you, ye shall ask what ye will, and it shall be done unto you.

JOHN 15:7

(15) It is the source of <u>spiritual victory</u>:

And take the helmet of salvation, and the word of the Spirit, which is the word of God.

EPHESIANS 6:17

I have written unto you, fathers, because ye have known him that is from the beginning. I have written unto you, young men, because ye are strong, and the word of God abideth in you, and ye have overcome the wicked one.

1 JOHN 2:14

(16) It is the source of <u>healing</u>:

My son, attend to my words; incline thine ear unto my sayings. Let them not depart from thine eyes; keep them in the midst of thine heart. For they are life unto those that find them, and health to all their flesh.

PROVERBS 4:20-22

He sent his word, and healed them, and delivered them from their destructions.

PSALM 107:20

(17) It is the source of <u>assurance</u>:

These things have I written unto you that believe on the name of the Son of God; that ye may know that ye have eternal life, and that ye may believe on the name of the Son of God.

1 JOHN 5:13

(18) It is the source of <u>joy</u>:

The statutes of the Lord are right, rejoicing the heart: the commandment of the Lord is pure, enlightening the eyes.

PSALM 19:8

Thy testimonies have I taken as an heritage for ever: for they are the rejoicing of my heart.

PSALM 119:111

(19) It is the source of <u>preparation for good works</u>:

All scripture is given by inspiration of God, and is profitable for doctrine, for reproof, for correction, for instruction in righteousness: That the man of God may be perfect, thoroughly furnished unto all good works.

2 TIMOTHY 3:16-17

(20) It is the source of <u>warning</u>:

Now all these things happened unto them for ensamples: and they are written for our admonition, upon whom the ends of the world are come.

1 CORINTHIANS 10:11

Types of Heart Conditions

1. Brokenhearted:

The LORD is nigh unto them that are of a broken heart; and saveth such as be of a contrite spirit.

PSALM 34:18

He healeth the broken in heart, and bindeth up their wounds.

PSALM 147:3

Reproach hath broken my heart; and I am full of heaviness: and I looked for some to take pity, but there was none; and for comforters, but I found none. They gave me, also gall for my meat; and in my thirst they gave me vinegar to drink.

PSALM 69:20-21

The Spirit of the Lord God is upon me; because the Lord hath anointed me to preach good tidings unto the meek; he hath sent me to bind up the brokenhearted to proclaim liberty to the captives, and the opening of the prison to them that are bound; To proclaim the acceptable year of the Lord.

ISAIAH 61:1-2

The Spirit of the Lord is upon me, because he hath anointed me to preach the gospel to the poor; he hath sent me to heal the brokenhearted, to preach deliverance to the captives, and recovering of sight to the blind, to set at liberty them that are bruised, To preach the acceptable year of the Lord.

LUKE 4:18-19

In an article from Misfit Ministries[3] written December 25, 2019, they address in detail, the meaning of the word *brokenhearted* in both Hebrew and Greek.

What Does the Word 'Brokenhearted' Mean In Hebrew and Greek?

If you've ever experienced a broken heart, you know there's nothing like it. You really feel a pain in your chest that hurts so deep. Your entire life gets thrown out of whack and it's difficult to find any good reason to get out of bed. It can feel like you've hit a roadblock and you just can't figure out how to get back on track. I wanted to look at what the Bible says about broken-heartedness and find out what does the word brokenhearted mean in Hebrew and Greek.

What "Brokenhearted" Means in Hebrew?

The Hebrew language combines two words to describe the broken-hearted just like we do. The two words they combine are *shabar* and *leb*.

shabar = to burst

---

3 Misfit Ministries

Shabar is the common word typically used to describe the breaking of things. It's used to tell the breaking of the following things:

- Bows (Hosea 1:5)
- Bones (Exodus 12:46)
- Earthen vessels (Judges 7:20)
- Swords (Hosea 2:18)
- Yokes or bonds (Jeremiah 28:10)

Also, this word is used to describe a shattered heart or emotion (Psalm 69:20; Ezekiel 6:9).

leb = feelings, will, intellect; the center of anything

This word is translated into 'heart' 508 times.

The heart of man includes the:

- Feelings
- Motives
- Affections
- Desires
- Will
- Aims
- Principles
- Thoughts
- Intellect

This term speaks of the entire inner man. The head is never regarded as the seat of intelligence. The heart is the center of all feelings and thoughts and the sources of all actions. It's also receptive to influence coming from the outer world and from God.

The Bible uses this term to speak of the organ (Exodus 2:8), the middle part of something (Exodus 15:8), a man's personality (Genesis 17:17), and the seat of emotions (Deuteronomy 6:5).

Since it's the seat of emotions, the Bible describes fearful hearts, merry hearts, and hearts that tremble. The heart is the resting place of the moral character and conscience of a person. For example, pride and rebellion abide in the heart.

The word of God also teaches that the Lord can give a new heart and create a clean one (Psalm 51:10).

> *A new heart also will I give you, and a new spirit will I put within you; and I will take the away the stony heart out of your flesh, and I will give you an heart of flesh.*
>
> Ezekiel 36:26

What "Brokenhearted" Means in Greek?

Just like in the previous language, the Greek also uses two words to describe the term *brokenhearted*. The two words we are going to look at are *suntribo* and *kardia*.

Suntribo = the crush completely; to shatter

This term is used to speak of harm done by a quick blow. It speaks of breaking something into pieces by crushing.

Kardia = the heart; the thoughts or feelings (mind).

The heart is the seat of:

Joy:

> *And ye now therefore have sorrow: but I will see you again, and your heart shall rejoice, and your joy no man taketh from you.*
>
> John 16:22

Grief:

> *That I have great heaviness and continual sorrow in my heart.*
>
> Romans 9:2

Moral nature and spiritual life:

> *For the life of the flesh is in the blood: and I have given it to you upon the altar to make an atonement for your souls: for it is the blood that maketh an atonement for the soul.*
>
> LEVITICUS 17:11

Physical life:

> *Nevertheless he left not himself without witness, in that he did good, and gave us rain from heaven, and fruitful seasons, filling our hearts with food and gladness.*
>
> ACTS 14:17

The thoughts:

> *For the word of God is quick, and powerful, and sharper than any twoedged sword, piercing even to the dividing asunder of soul and spirit, and of the joints and marrow, and is a discerner of the thoughts and intents of the heart.*
>
> HEBREWS 4:12

The perceptions:

> *He hath blinded their eyes, and hardened their heart; that they should not see with their eyes, nor understand with their heart, and be converted, and I should heal them.*
>
> JOHN 12:40

The understanding:

> *Because that, when they knew God, they glorified him not as God, neither were thankful; but became vain in their imaginations and their foolish heart was darkenedd.*
>
> ROMANS 1:21

The imagination:

> *He hath shewed strength with his arm; he hath scattered the proud in the imagination of their hearts.*
>
> LUKE 1:51

The reasoning powers:

> *But there were certain of the scribes sitting there, and reasoning in their hearts.*
>
> MARK 2:6

Conscience:

> *For if our heart condemn us, God is greater than our heart, and knoweth all things.*
>
> 1 JOHN 3:20

Purpose:

> *Every man according as he purposeth in his heart, so let him give; not grudgingly, or of necessity: for God loveth a cheerful giver.*
>
> 2 CORINTHIANS 9:7

Intentions:

> *Forasmuch then as Christ hath suffered for us in the flesh, arm yourselves likewise with the same mind: for he that hath suffered in the flesh hath ceased from sin;*
>
> 1 PETERS 4:1

Faith:

> *For with the heart man believeth unto righteousness; and with the mouth confession is made unto salvation.*
>
> ROMANS 10:10

The will:

> *And let the peace of God rule in your hearts, to the which also ye are called in one body; and be ye thankful.*
>
> COLOSSIANS 3:15

The desires:

> *But I say unto you, That whosoever looketh on a woman to lust after her hath committed adultery with her already in his heart.*
>
> MATTHEWS 5:28

The affections:

> *And they said one to another, Did not our heart burn within us, while he talked with us by the way and while he opened to us the scriptures?*
>
> LUKE 24:32

2. Circumcised:

> *For he is not a Jew, which is one outwardly; neither is that circumcision, which is outward in the flesh: But he is a Jew, which is one inwardly; and circumcision is that of the heart, in the spirit, and not in the letter; whose praise is not of men, but of God.*
>
> ROMANS 2:28-29

> *For we are the circumcision, which worship God in the spirit, and rejoice in Christ Jesus, and have no confidence in the flesh.*
>
> PHILIPPIANS 3:3

Dake[4] explains "A true Jew is not the one who is circumcised in the flesh, neither is true circumcision in the flesh. A true Jew is one that has inward circumcision of the heart and in the spirit and has more than an outward cutting in the flesh and a profession of truth." This does not teach that every Christian is a Jew, but to be a true Jew one must be of the seed of Abraham, and have circumcision of the heart, and be a child of the promise.

There are four points here regarding the circumcision:

1. The true circumcision is of the heart and in the spirit,
2. We are worshippers in spirit as John 4:24 states that *"God is a Spirit: and they that worship him must worship him in spirit and in truth"*,
3. We rejoice in Christ and should be able to find our happiness in Him,
4. Our confidence in Christ is manifest by our demonstration of our belief in Him by the Spirit and not by the flesh.

3. **Clean:**

   Create in me a clean heart, O God; and renew a right spirit within me.

   PSALM 51:10

   Truly God is good to Israel, even to such as are of a clean heart.

   PSALM 73:1

   Who can say, I have made my heart clean, I am pure from my sin?

   PROVERBS 20:9

---

4 Dake page 282

Psalm 51:10 outlines the process in which one can receive a clean heart. First you must ask in sincerity that your sins to be forgiven; then God will create a new heart that will include a right spirit within. With that renewing you can expect the following:

a.   You have been forgiven of your sins and your sinful records has been wiped clean.
b.   You have developed a new way of thinking that is pure and not dishonest, resentful, or full of pride.
c.   You endeavor to please God and your actions demonstrate that.

There is no one that exist who can say they themselves are responsible for the cleansing of their own heart; or who has totally and without question been completely purified from all sin. Only those who have accepted Jesus Christ as their Lord and Savior are truthfully able to say, they have been cleansed by the blood of Christ.

According to the Old Testament, saints were cleansed, purified from sin, and received full redemptive from sin only because of their faith in the Redeemer who was to come.

4.   Compassionate/Merciful/Kind/Sympathetic/Tender:
Put on therefore, as the elect of God, holy and beloved, bowels of mercies, kindness, humbleness of mind, meekness, longsuffering; Forbearing one another, and forgiving one another, if any man have a quarrel against any, even as Christ forgave you, so also do ye. And above all these things put on charity, which is the bond of perfectness.
COLOSSIANS 3:12-14

The Lord is merciful and gracious, slow to anger, and plenteous in mercy.

PSALM 103:8

Finally, be ye all of one mind, having compassion one of another, love as brethren, be pitiful, be courteous.

1 PETER 3:8

How do you obtain a compassionate heart? Or the importance of having a compassionate heart.

According to the Merriam-Webster website, the definition of compassion is the "sympathetic consciousness of others' distress together with a desire to alleviate it." The *New Oxford American Dictionary* defines compassion as a "sympathetic, pity and concern for the sufferings or misfortune of others."

Learning where the word comes from has its importance in that the Latin root for the word *compassion* is "pati" which means to suffer, while the prefix of *com-* means with. So, then the word compassion in a literal sense means to suffer with or share in the pain and suffering of another. Compassion is closely related to the word empathy, as being empathetic is the ability to imagine another person's plight or pain. Both words share some meaning in that they both are based on emotions and feelings, which in turn can cause various types of "mercy" to be shown through the actions of those who are moved with a sense of compassion and/or empathy. Although the Bible does not actually define the word compassion, but rather shows us what that characteristic looks like or how it is displayed in or demonstrated by someone. The best way to know what a compassionate heart is, and how it's applied, is to follow the examples of Christ.

There are several scriptures that give credence to those examples:

And Jesus went about all the cities and villages, teaching in their synagogues, and preaching the gospel of the kingdom, and healing every sickness and every disease among the people. But when he saw the multitudes, he was moved with compassion on them, because they fainted, and were scattered abroad, as sheep having no shepherd.

MATTHEW 9:35-36

So Jesus had compassion on them, and touched their eyes: and immediately their eyes received sight, and they followed him.

MATTHEW 20:34

Who can have compassion on the ignorant, and on them that are out of the way; for that he himself also is compassed with infirmity.

HEBREWS 5:2

But whoso hath this world's good, and seeth his brother have need, and shutteth up his bowels of compassion from him, how dwelleth the love of God in him? My little children, let us not love in word, neither in tongue, but in deed and in truth.

1 JOHN 3:17-18

An article posted by Elizabeth Peale Allen[5] on August 22, 2014, shows that those examples of Christ's compassion have two things in common:

1. Jesus notices the people around him which tells us that compassion is only possible when we are attuned

---

5 Elizabeth Peale Allen

to others. If we are absorbed in our own feelings, problems, worries, and desires, we will overlook the needs of those God put in our path and ignore the opportunity to help them.

2. Jesus responds to people, instead of reacting to them. He listens to the ten lepers rather than being irritated that they're interrupting his conversation. He takes time to speak with the woman who touches the hem of his garment, instead of simply chastising her for lacking appropriate boundaries.

Elizabeth also gives three basic steps we can take that will help us get better at having compassion when we practice showing it:

1. **Build up your empathy:**
    Spend five minutes a day practicing putting yourself in someone else's shoes. Choose a news report, a neighbor, or a member of your own family, and really contemplate what it feels like to be that person. Don't shy away as soon as you think, that must be awful. Delve deep into what it's like to suffer in that way. This exercise can help you learn to "Rejoice with those who rejoice; mourn with those who mourn" (Romans 12:15).

2. **Learn to pause before speaking:**
    Scripture tells us, "People look at the outward appearance, but the Lord looks at the heart" (1 Samuel 16:7). To be compassionate towards others, we need to allow time for the Holy Spirit to override our tendency to judge. A simple prayer like, "Holy Spirit, guide my heart," often provides enough space (and

guidance!) to help us see why people are behaving the way they are.

3. **Recognize the barriers to compassion:**
It's impossible to be annoyed and compassionate at the same time. Frustration, suspicion, irritation, bitterness, dislike, and anger are all signs that may be looking at others without compassion. We can pray to the Father, "Get rid of all bitterness, rage and anger, brawling and slander, along with every form of malice," that rules in our hearts (Ephesians 4:31). Ask God to help you to be kind and tenderhearted (Ephesians 4:32). Begin this very day to cultivate a spirit of compassion

5. **Contrite:**
The sacrifices of God are a broken spirit: a broken and a contrite heart, O God, thou wilt not despise.

PSALM 51:17

God will not look down upon a broken and contrite spirit or heart because of the tremendous amount of mercy and grace promised to those are beaten down and crushed by the drudges of sin and satanic pressures.

An article titled, "How Can We Embrace a Contrite Heart and Spirit?" written by Stephanie Englehart[6] speaks to this subject at length as she defines what Psalm 51:17 means to have a broken spirit and a contrite heart.

---

6 Stephanie Englehart

"What Does Psalm 51:17 Mean by a Broken Spirit and A Contrite Heart Definition?

To have a contrite spirit means we feel guilt or remorse over our wrongdoing and seek repentance in place of our sin. This is exemplified in Psalm 51 as King David laments and repents over his sin in 2 Samuel 11-12:14. David wrote this Psalm just after Nathan the prophet confronted him about sleeping with Bathsheba, impregnating her, and arranging her husband, Uriah's, murder. David's sin was great, but as Psalm 51:1 states, Gods mercy is abundant.

The confessional prayer of this Psalm is deeply personal for David, but its instructional elements provide a framework for how we, as believers, are to have a broken spirit and contrite heart. The Psalm is best read as a whole, not focusing solely on verse 17, but taking all 19 verses into context. As you read through the Psalm, you will find a few key elements that explain what it means to have a broken spirit and contrite heart.

A Broken Spirit and Contrite Heart Means We Are Humble Before God

The Psalm opens with an appeal to God for mercy and forgiveness. David's plea for God's steadfast love points to our need for humility before God. As David openly admits his sin, he confesses God's mercy is not something he deserve but desires. David does not spend his time looking inward for the answer or solution to his problem but humbles himself by looking outward toward God and His promises.

A broken spirit and contrite heart mean we come humbly before God, acknowledging our sins, and proclaiming God's goodness. This form of humble spirit expresses our need for God and His salvation alone. It does not blame God or others for our sins, but rather, takes full responsibility for the actions we took. As we humble ourselves before

God, we recognize and become dependent upon His mercy. This both kills the pride that God opposes within us and maximizes the mercy of God as the one who deserves the glory.

A Broken Spirit and Contrite Heart Means We Remorse Over Grieving the Lord

David did not treat his sin like my preschool aged children and their indispensable sharing shenanigans. Psalm 51:3 describes David as having his sin ever before him. He feels such guilt over what he has done, and places responsibility on the proper party—himself. In verse 4, David continues to proclaim that he has sinned only against God. He is fully aware that his actions have hurt others, but points to the idea that God is the ultimate judge of all sin, and that sin grieves the Lord (Ephesians 4:30).

A Broken Spirit and Contrite Heart Means We Turn Toward God

David may have experienced a guilt-ridden heart, but he didn't sit in the guilt and shame of his sin, past repentance. David found the correlation between being satisfied in the grace of God and rejoicing in his salvation. Psalm 51:7-14 describes the process of repentance clearly. David acknowledges his sin and asks God to hide his face from his guilt. He asks God for a renewed spirit, and clean heart, and asks God to restore the joy of his salvation. In his quest for deliverance, he describes the response of a redeemed sinner. A broken spirit and contrite heart mean we repent of our sin by turning away from our disobedient actions, admitting our mistakes, and turning towards God.

Repentance does not end with us sitting in guilt and shame over the sins we have committed forever. Repentance is the act of remembering *who* our salvation comes from and turning towards God's steadfast love and mercy. The goal of true repentance is not shame based fear or self-deprecation, but to be restored into the joy of salvation. As we see the mighty hand of mercy saving us, we can have no other response than great joy.

The question has also been asked: How does it benefit God for us to possess a broken spirit and contrite hearts? The answer can be found in Isaiah 57:15:

> *"For thus saith the high and lofty One that inhabiteth eternity, whose name is Holy. I dwell in the high and holy place, with him also that is of a contrite and humble spirit, to revive the spirit of the humble, and to revive the heart of the contrite ones."*

> *The Lord is nigh unto them that are of a broken heart; and saveth such as be of a contrite spirit.*
>
> PSALM 34:18

God wants us to know that He is well satisfied and content when He witnesses a humble spirit. He watches for a spirit that demonstrates their remorse is authentic. He causes the veil of deceit to be removed from our eyes so we can see how hardened our hearts have become. Our response to His call to turn from a life of evil and wickedness and allow ourselves to become renewed according to His will for us is rewarded with His mercy and grace toward us.

Understanding the grace that God extends to us will also lead us to a place where we no longer want to walk in sinfulness; but have a deep desire for God's love to reach us as He bestows upon us the many benefits stored up for that time. We find that we can come to God without being condemned as we seek to find a hiding place in Him. He meets us where we can find love, healing, and a permanent place of solace.

The Lord is nigh unto them that are of a broken heart; and saveth such as be of a contrite spirit.

PSALM 34:18

He health the broken in heart, and bindeth up their wounds.

PSALM 147:3

Likewise, ye younger, submit yourselves unto the elder. Yea, all of you be subject one to another, and be clothed with humility, for God resisteth the proud, and giveth grace to the humble.

1 PETER 5:5

For thus saith the high and lofty One that inhabiteth eternity, whose name is Holy; I dwell in the high and holy place, with him also that is of a contrite and humble spirit, to revive the spirit of the humble, and to revive the heart of the contrite ones.

ISAIAH 57:15

6. Fear of God Heart

And unto man he said, Behold, the fear of the Lord, that is wisdom; and to depart from evil is understanding.

JOB 28:28

The Lord is exalted; for he dwelleth on high: he hath filled Zion with judgment and righteousness. And wisdom and knowledge shall be the stability of thy times, and strength of salvation: the fear of the Lord is his treasure.

ISAIAH 33:5-6

The fear of the Lord is the beginning of knowledge: but fools despise wisdom and instruction.

PROVERBS 1:7

The fear of the Lord prolongeth days: but the years of the wicked shall be shortened.

PROVERBS 10:27

Praise ye the Lord. Blessed is the man that feareth the Lord, that delighteth greatly in his commandments. His seed shall be mighty upon earth: the generation of the upright shall be blessed.

PSALM 112:1-2

In the fear of the Lord is strong confidence: and his children shall have a place of refuge. The fear of the Lord is a fountain of life, to depart from the snares of death.

PROVERBS 14:26-27

An article by Mark D. Roberts, "The Stability of Your Times"[7] gives a clear, easy to understand commentary on Isaiah 33:5-6. "In times that feel so uncertain and shaky, do you yearn for some stability?"

"I expect your answer to this question is "Yes." That's my answer, to be sure. And that would be the answer of most people. As you may recall, in (another) devotion, I referred to a psychological study that shows human beings prefer certainty over uncertainty even when that certainty is negative. If we know something bad is coming our way, at least we can prepare for it. If we are uncertain, we're stuck in anxiety.

---

7 Mark D. Roberts

But, in a word that's continually changing, in which the only predictability is unpredictability, true stability is elusive. Oh, if we're blessed with a fair amount of power and possessions, we can provide the semblance of stability for our lives. We might even think we have made everything in life predictably stable. But when something comes along like an automobile accident, a cancer diagnosis, or a worldwide pandemic and our stability turns out to be more romantic than real. Yes, as they say, we live in uncertain times. Considering this fact, we wonder: Will we ever experience the stability of our times?

The Bible answers these questions with an affirmation that speaks to the yearning of our souls. When Isaiah 33:5-6 speaks to the "stability of your times," what does it mean?

The prophecy in Isaiah 33 came to God's people in difficult if not uncertain times. An unidentified destroyer, probably some nation with superior military power, was threatening Israel. So, the prophet cried out, *"O Lord, be gracious to us; we wait for you. Be our arm every morning, our salvation in times of trouble"* (Isaiah 33:2). The Hebrew word translated here as "times" is 'et. That word appears again four verses later in the phrase, "he will be the stability of your times" (Isaiah 33:6). The context makes it clear that this does not mean God's people will never go through hard times. Rather, during those times God offers "justice and righteousness...abundance of salvation, wisdom, and knowledge (Isaiah 33:5-6). 'Zion's treasure' is not protection from all difficulties. Rather it is "the fear of the Lord" (Isaiah 33:6). It is the relationship we have with God who is utterly trustworthy, utterly gracious, utterly wise, utterly knowing.

When our times feel certain, when things are going as we had planned, it's easy to trust in our circumstances or our own ability to control them. But in uncertain times, we recognize our own limitations.

We realize just how much we need God to be "the stability of our times." Only in Him will we find a solid, trustworthy foundation on which to build our lives."

Psalm 112:2-9 outlines the benefits that those who walk in righteousness are positioned to receive when they demonstrate a healthy fear of the Lord as follows:

- His children shall be mighty on earth (verse 2)
- They shall be blessed
- They shall be wealthy (verse 3)
- They shall be eternally righteous (verses 3, 9)
- They shall have light in darkness (verse 4)
- They are gracious
- They are full of compassion
- They are righteous
- They show favor through their giving to others (verse 5)
- They guide their own affairs with discretion
- They shall not be moved eternally (verse 6)
- They shall be remembered forever
- They shall not fear evil news, but believes the report of the Lord (verse 7)
- Their hearts stayed fixed on God
- Their trust is wholly in God
- Their hearts are established as they remain steadfast (verse 8)
- They shall not be afraid or fear evil
- They shall see the defeat of their enemies
- They are generous (verse 9)
- They are merciful and good
- Their horn shall be exalted

7. **Fixed:**

I sought the Lord, and he heard me, and delivered me from all my fears.

PSALM 34:4

My heart is fixed, O God, my heart is fixed: I will sing and give praise.

PSALM 57:7

He shall not be afraid of evil tidings: his heart is fixed, trusting in the Lord. His heart is established, he shall not be afraid, until he sees his desire upon his enemies.

PSALM 112:7-8

Many blessings await those whose hearts are fixed on God, and who fear Him. They can expect:
   a.   Prayers answered
   b.   To prosper
   c.   Wants and needs supplied
   d.   Be delivered from fear
   5.   Receive redemption

When we keep our hearts fixed on Him, and fear God because of His reverence, He is just to deliver[8] us from the 14 kinds of fear as following:
   1.   Fear of man (Hebrews 13:6l; Luke 12:5)
   2.   Death (Hebrews 2:15)
   3.   The future (Genesis 46:3)

---

8 Dake Page 928

4. Danger (Exodus 14:13)
5. Idol gods (Judges 6:10; 2 Kings 17:25-38)
6. Dreams (Job 4:14-16)
7. Evil (Psalm 23:4; Proverbs 1:33)
8. War (Psalm 27:3)
9. Nothing-imaginative fear (Psalms 53:5)
10. Enemies (Psalm 118:6)
11. Punishment (Proverbs 1:26-27)
12. Darkness (Colossians 1:13)
13. Ghosts (Matthews 14:26)
14. Spirit of fear (2 Timothy 1:6-7)

These scriptures are references to the characteristics of those walking in righteousness and have been condemned and persecuted by others. Having a fixed heart shows the state of the heart and mind of one who fears the Lord and who follow His commandments. We should continue to seek Him, trust Him, and praise Him.

8. Heart after God's own Heart

And when he had removed him, he raised up unto them David to be their king; to whom also he gave testimony, and said, I have found David the son of Jesse, a man after mine own heart, which shall fulfil all my will.

ACTS 13:22

But the Lord said unto Samuel, look not on his countenance, or on the height of his stature; because I have refused him: for the Lord seeth; for man looketh on the outward appearance, but the Lord looketh on the heart.

1 SAMUEL 16:7

The Lord search the heart, I try the reins, even to give every man according to his ways, and according to the fruit of his doings.

JEREMIAH 17:10

In an article written by Ron Edmonson, he gives ten reasons why David is called, **"A Man After God's Own Heart:"**[9]

Acts 13:22 says, *"After removing Saul, he made David their king. He testified concerning him: 'I have found David son of Jesse a man after my own heart; he will do everything I want him to do.'"*

The following words describe the heart of David as seen in his own writings:

1. **Humble** – Lowborn men are but a breath, the highborn are but a lie; if weighed on a balance, they are nothing; together they are only a breath. Psalm 62:9 (NIV)
2. **Reverent** – I call to the Lord, who is worthy of praise, and I am saved from my enemies. Psalm 18:3 (NIV)
3. **Respectful** – Be merciful to me, O Lord, for I am in distress; my eyes grow weak with sorrow, my soul and my body with grief. Psalm 31:9 (NIV)
4. **Trusting** – TThe LORD is my light and my salvation— whom shall I fear? The LORD is the stronghold of my life—of whom shall I be afraid? Psalm 27:1 (NIV)
5. **Loving** – I love you, O Lord, my strength. Psalm 18:1 (NIV)
6. **Devoted** – You have filled my heart with greater joy than when their grain and new wine abound. Psalm 4:7 (NIV)

---

9 Ron Edmonson

7. **Recognition** – I will praise you, O Lord, with all my heart; I will tell of all your wonders. Psalm 9:1 (NIV)
8. **Faithful** – Surely goodness and love will follow me all the days of my life, and I will dwell in the house of the LORD forever. Psalm 23:6 (NIV)
9. **Obedient** – Give me understanding, and I will keep your law and obey it with all my heart. Psalm 119:34 (NIV)
10. **Repentant** – For the sake of your name, O Lord, forgive my iniquity, though it is great. Psalm 25:11 (NIV)

Although David disappointed God many times, and was not a perfect man, he still provides a good example for how we should govern ourselves. David often looked within himself and examined his own loyalty and dedication to God. He possessed a sense of humbleness that caused him to evaluate his integrity, obedience, and moral compass. David was meticulous in doing an inward analysis of his own heart to assess whether he continued to reach for the perfection he knew God was looking for.

David's example is a great road map for how we are to live our life in that he was swift to recognize his failings and submitted to a sincere repentance for his sins. He went to God often to ask for forgiveness as he looked forward to God to keep His promises. David's trust in God allowed him to remain open to God's instruction which is why he has always been referred to as a man after God's own heart.

And Samuel said to Saul, Thou hast done foolishly: thou has not kept the commandment of the Lord thy God, which he commanded thee: for now would the Lord have established thy kingdom upon Israel for ever. But now thy kingdom shall not continue: the Lord hath sought him a man after his own heart, and the Lord hath commanded him to be captain over his people, because thou hast not kept that which the Lord commanded thee.

1 SAMUEL 13:13-14

Every way of a man is right in his own eyes, but the Lord pondereth the hearts.

PROVERBS 21:2

9. Honest and Good:

Now the parable is this: The seed is in the word of God. Those by the way side are they that hear; then cometh the devil, and taketh away the word out of their hearts, lest they should believe and be saved. They on the rock are they, which, when they hear, receive the word with joy; and these have no root, which for a while believe, and in time of temptation fall away. And that which fell among thorns are they, which, when they have heard, go forth, and are choked with cares and riches and pleasures of this life, and bring no fruit to perfection. But that on the good ground are they, which in an honest and good heart, having heard the word, keep it, and bring forth fruit with patience,

LUKE 8:11-15

This scripture addresses the Parable of the Sower in verses 8:11 through 15, which focuses on what dictates what an "honest and good" heart is made up of. It is one that once heard, plants the truth of God's word inside, to trust and rely upon daily. This requires a level of faith that is unwavering, and often answered through Apostle Paul's scripture in Romans 10:17:

So then faith cometh by hearing, and hearing by the word of God.

That scripture is proceeded by verses. 14-16:

How then shall they call on him in whom they have not believed? And how shall they believe in him of whom they have not heard? And how shall they hear without a preacher? And how shall they preach, except they be sent? As it is written. How beautiful are the feet of them that preach the gospel of peace, and bring glad tidings of good things. But they have not all obeyed the gospel. For Esaias saith, Lord, who hath believed our report?

That scripture outlines the 7 know-how steps to receiving that level of gospel faith needed to ensure God's word is planted in our hearts and to understand how it is essential to our faith walk.:

1. The gospel given by Christ (verse 14)
2. The gospel must be preached (verse 14)
3. A preacher is necessary (verse 14)
4. The preacher must be sent (verse 15)
5. The gospel must be heard (verses 14–15)
6. The gospel must be believed (verse 16)
7. The gospel must be obeyed (verses 9–17)

For this cause also thank we God without ceasing, because, when ye received the word of God which ye heard of us, ye received it not as the word of men, but as it is in truth, the word of God, which effectually worketh also in you that believed.

1 Thessalonians 2:13

Getting to a place where we can worship God in spirit and in truth requires practice, dedication, and faithfulness. The "word of God" which is the "seed" must be "planted" and "received" in good soil that is subject to grow and produce fruit. For God's word to thrive, it must first survive and be nourished before it can bear fruit. It will not become effective if it is suffocated and not fed daily. An honest and good heart remains open for growth; a heart whose growth is not stunted or bogged down by daily cares and worries.

An honest and good heart will receive the word of God as being truth and not words that are made up or fabricated. And lets us know from our experiences, the word has been effective, and the results produced are proof that leads us to believe in its truth. An honest and good heart will read the word of God—the Bible—and be steadfast in believing the good news that it contains. That process with allow us to develop an indisputable faith in His promises and build strength as we walk in the fruit of the spirit. We should pursue an atmosphere of worship with others as we fellowship together and endeavor to worship God in spirit and in truth.

10. Joyful or Glad:

A merry heart maketh a cheerful countenance: but by sorrow of the heart the spirit is broken. The heart of him that hath understanding seeketh knowledge: but the mouth of fools feedeth on foolishness.

PROVERBS 15:13-14

These things have I spoken unto you, that my joy might remain in you, and that your joy might be full.

JOHN 15:11

The Lord is my strength and my shield; my heart trusted in him, and I am helped therefore my heart greatly rejoiceth; and with my song will I praise him.

PSALM 28:7

For thou, Lord, hast made me glad through thy work: I will triumph in the works of thy hands.

PSALM 92:4

And the ransomed of the Lord shall return, and come in Zion with songs and everlasting joy upon their heads: they shall obtain joy and gladness, and sorrow and sighing shall flee away.

ISAIAH 35:10

And ye now therefore have sorrow: but I will see you again, and your heart shall rejoice, and your joy no man taketh from you.

JOHN 16:22

Through scriptures, we are encouraged to be glad, merry, cheerful, and joyful for many reasons.

When we have faith and trust in God, we can experience His blessings and gain access to all His benefits. Here's six ways to know if you are allowing joy and gladness to fill your heart:

1. The person with a joyful and glad heart will trust in God with all their heart. We learn to look beyond our trials and tribulations that may befall us from time to time; embracing the confidence we have in Him that He will perform what He says in His Holy Word.

2. The person who has a joyful heart finds a time and place or prayer closet for his/her personal time with God. His Word says He will never leave us or forsake us, even when we don't feel His presence, we know He is near.

3. The person with a joyful heart is thankful for all of God's benefits daily. We acknowledge what we have, we don't focus on what we don't have.

4. The person with a joyful heart, studies the Word, and is obedient to His word. We study to show ourselves approved; a workman not ashamed as they rightly divide the word of truth.

5. The person with a joyful heart knows the difference between having joy or having momentary sadness in our lives. Joy and gladness can accelerate above the sadness and find an inner peace.

6. The person with a joyful heart is confident is knowing God will direct their path and maneuver through whatever maize life may present. (Psalms 16:11)

11. Meek and lowly:

Come unto me, all ye that labour and are heavy laden, and I will give you rest. Take my yoke upon you, and learn from me; for I am meek and lowly in heart: and ye shall find rest unto your souls. For my yoke is easy, and my burden is light.

MATTHEW 11:28-30

Some of the most powerful and beloved words in the New Testament offer relief to those who accept the invitation of Christ to walk in discipleship and follow him. This invitation comes in five parts that if not read and studied carefully, might otherwise be overlooked. Four of those parts are from an article outlined in Bible.org[10] and each word is broken down in detail:

A. **The Commanding Invitation (11:28a): "Come unto me, all ye who are weary and heavy laden;"**

In this section of scripture, the word Come is coming from the passionate heart of Jesus Christ our Lord and Savior and is being expressed with a strong sense of appeal that should also be taken as a non-negotiable command or directive. For believers, it is "a call" to follow him as a committed disciple; a call to turn their lives over to Him. For those who have not accepted Christ, it's a call to believe in Him.

The word, "unto" indicates an opportunity to establish an unguarded relationship with Him.

The word, *me* shows the desire for Jesus to make this invitation personal; and implies He is open to this intimate fellowship.

The word, *all* shows how inclusive this invitation is to all and anyone who would be open to a more meaningful way of life for those who need relief.

The words, *who are weary* and *heavy laden* look into the specific conditions that one may be experiencing. There's no doubt He is speaking to instances where the trials and tribulations of life are and can be quite burdensome. *Weary* means to be overworked, fatigued, or exhausted to the point of giving up. *Heavy laden* is a form of carrying a load, or of being in a state of oppression and overbearing

---

10 Bible.org

when carried over a long period of time.

While they are not always visible, these troublesome times are likened to a load that has been placed on the back of an ox.

B. **The Promise with Purpose (11:28b): "And I will give you rest."**

The word, *I* again is personal and gives us a sense that He is waiting for us to establish that individual relationship before He can perform on our behalf. The word, *rest* implies receiving relief from labor; to unwind, being refreshed or able to experience comfort or calm after a time.

C. **The Direct Admonition (11:29a): "Take my yoke upon you, and learn from Me;"**

Here we have a warning to heed these words of counsel that will get us to the place of rest that has been promised. The word, *take* here means to decide by submitting to the Lord before we can get to the place of rest. In this sense, this is comparable to "take up your cross." *My yoke*, has a specific meaning here and is central to understanding what the significance of a *yoke* is. In this sense, we're talking about being "bound or harnessed" by the weight or oppressive loads or burdens that overwhelm us. Then we are given a directive to *learn* which means to experience through practice to the point of becoming a habit of application.

D. **The Motivation to Move (11:29b-30):**

In this portion of scripture, Jesus gives us a snapshot of his personality; He tells us a little about His character and what we can expect or achieve if we would adhere to His command. He tells us why our expectation can be higher than other admonitions and what we can garner because of our submission to His word.

"For I am meek and lowly in heart:" He says with certainty that following Him will lead to a path different than others we have followed without results. How we have allowed ourselves to be deceived by other masters who seek to lure us into a more sinful nature. But not with Him, for His heart is full of humility for us and His concern is genuine. "And ye shall find rest unto your souls."

The word, *easy* in this portion of scripture that reads, *"for my yoke is easy,"* tells us why we should take upon us this yoke. It tells us the value and usefulness of following this directive. It gives us a glimpse of not being fearful, but rather faithful in our submission to this concept. These words are followed with *"and my burden is light."* Even gives us a description of what we can expect or identify with. It says we can look forward to receiving what's likened to having a weight lifted from our shoulders.

E. **The Rewards of Rest, Truth, and Knowledge:**
There is great reward in becoming a disciple of Christ and following Him. He has promised and volunteered to be with us. To help lift those heavy loads that make our burdens lighter and more easily managed. Truth and knowledge in Jesus' commands assure us that when we submit to His authority, we are guaranteed to reap the benefits of that submission. This command is

personal to each one of us that makes the decision to "come unto Him," because each one of us are carrying different burdens; therefore, have a tailor-made yoke designed specifically for us as an individual. This God-given knowledge enables us to move forward throughout the circumstances of life with confidence and gratitude in the Savior who walks with us.

12. Melted:

And as soon as we had heard these things, our hearts did melt, neither did there remain any more courage in any man, because of you: for the Lord your God, he is God in heaven above, and in earth beneath.

JOSHUA 2:11

And it came to pass, when all the kings of the Amorites, which were on the side of Jordan westward, and all the kings of the Canaanites, which were by the sea, heard that the Lord had dried up the waters of Jordan from before the children of Israel, until we were passed over, that their heart melted, neither was there spirit in them any more, because of the children of Israel.

JOSHUA 5:1

Forty years old was I when Moses the servant of the Lord sent me from Kadeshbarnea to espy out the land; and I brought him word again as it was in mine heart. Nevertheless my brethren that went up with me made the heart of the people melt: but I wholly followed the Lord my God.

JOSHUA 14:7-8

This is all in response to hearing the testimonies of the miracles God had performed on behalf of the Israelites. And knowing this can be expected when faith in the promises of God is in the heart which makes all things possible where without faith, they are impossible. The word, "melted" in Joshua 2:11 indicate a spirit of fear, of reservation, in distrust of what God has promised. It shows a lack of confidence in what we should know to be true but have allowed our minds to deceive our hearts and be influenced by doubt in times of what appears to be uncertainty.

> *If any of you lack wisdom, let him ask of God, that giveth to all men liberally, and upbraideth not; and it shall be given him. But let him ask in faith, nothing wavering. For he that wavereth is like a wave of the sea driven with the wind and tossed. For let not that man think that he shall receive anything of the Lord. A double minded man is unstable in all his ways.*
>
> JAMES 1:5-6

Another word or term for fear is doubt. Here we are admonished to be steadfast, unmovable, and always abounding in the word of the Lord. To shun the urge to rise like a wave one minute and sink the next minute. We should refrain from the doubt that seeks to dissuade us from the assurances we have in our hearts that God's word never fails. A man who lacks faith and doubts is not positioned to get an answer from God.

13. Merry:

> *A merry heart maketh a cheerful countenance: but by sorrow of the heart the spirit is broken. The heart of him that hath understanding seeketh knowledge: but the mouth of fools*

feedeth on foolishness. All the days of the afflicted are evil: but he that is of a merry heart hath a continual feast.

PROVERBS 15:13-15,

A merry heart doeth good like a medicine: but a broken spirit drieth the bones

PROVERBS 17:22

These scriptures show the contrast between one with a merry heart, and one with an evil heart. Focus should be on those with a joyful temperament as opposed to one who displays a dark or oppressive spirit. It also highlights some of the characteristics between a wise man who seeks knowledge and one who feeds on foolishness.

These scripture gives an indication of the following conditions that are in contrast:

- When the state of mind of one who is satisfied, it will show visibly on the outside. You will be able to see the sparkle or glimmer in their eye or the radiant shine on their face. Happiness has an outward characteristic, while those who generate grief or sorrow can cause the spirit to be broken. Sorrow affects the inner parts as it tears down the natural resiliency of the body, which can bring despair.
- Those who hold merriment in their hearts will also seek wisdom and knowledge, while those who are foolish will allow foolishness to flow from their mouths.
- Those with a merry heart will be calm, self-controlled, and aware of God's glory, all while being obedient to His voice and commands, while those who are evil will show their distress at how miserable they are.

In the meaning of Proverbs 17:22, the following is evident:

- Having a merry heart equates to walking in a godly manner and shows it adds to both the spiritual and physical health. When sickness present itself, a merry heart can bring healing and recovery at a faster pace.
- A merry heart is like taking medicine to feel better when the body is sick or ailing. We can choose for ourselves whether we're going to be in misery, or if we're going to maintain a joyful heart.
- Having a broken spirit can physically affect the conditions of our bones. There is actually a "drying-up" effect when we allow our spirits to be down or depressed.

14. New Heart, A Stony Heart, and Heart of Flesh:

Therefore I will judge you, O house of Israel, every one according to his ways, saith the Lord GOD. Repent, and turn yourselves from all your transgressions; so iniquity shall not be your ruin. Cast away from you all your transgressions, whereby ye have transgressed; and make you a new heart and a new spirit: for why will ye die, O house of Israel? For I have no pleasure in the death of him that dieth, saith the Lord God: wherefore turn yourselves, and live ye.

EZEKIEL 18:30-32

Then will I sprinkle clean water upon you, and ye shall be clean: from all your filthiness, and from all your idols, will I cleanse you. A new heart also will I give you, and a new spirit will I put within you: and I will take away the stony heart out of your flesh, and I will give you an heart of flesh. And I will put my spirit within you, and cause you to walk in my statutes, and ye shall keep my judgments, and do them. And ye shall dwell in the land that I gave to your fathers; and ye shall be my people, and I will be your God.

EZEKIEL 36:25-28

Therefore if any man be in Christ, he is a new creature: old things are passed away; behold, all things are become new. And all things are of God, who hath reconciled us to himself by Jesus Christ, and hath given to us the ministry of reconciliation; To wit, that God in Christ, reconciling the world unto himself, not imputing their trespasses unto them; and hath committed unto us the word of reconciliation.

2 CORINTHIANS 5:17-18

And I will give them one heart, and I will put a new spirit within you; and I will take the stony heart out of their flesh, and will give them an heart of flesh:

EZEKIEL 11:19

The promises God extended were not just for Israel, but for all those who seek salvation. Upon meeting those conditions, He establishes that He will regather all of Israel, not only Judah, but all the tribes from the nations and bring them back to their own land to live forever under the Messiah. These things we can look forward to once we adhere to God's commands to turn from a walk that is not pleasing in His eyesight. As stated in the earlier scripture, God takes no pleasure in our suffering a death where there is no hope of our looking forward to an eternity with our Lord and Savior Jesus Christ who sits at the right hand of God.

The result of seeking conversion brings many blessings to include:
- Walking in God's statutes
- Keep and do His ordinances
- Shall be called the people of God
- He shall be their God

15. Perfect:

Let your heart therefore be perfect with the Lord our God, to walk in his statutes, and to keep his commandments, as at this day.

1 KINGS 8:61

Then the people rejoiced, for that they offered willingly, because with perfect heart they offered willingly to the Lord: and David the king also rejoiced with great joy.

1 CHRONICLES 29:9

There are several indications in 1 Kings 8:61 that God wants us to pursue perfection by participating in the following:
- As we walk in obedience, we should be able to show sincerity in our purpose.
- We should be able to demonstrate the keeping of the statutes He has given us by being fully committed to His commands.
- We should be able to show our devotion as we walk in the commandments God has laid out before us.
- To show our faithfulness as we worship God Almighty and not fall into idolatry as in days past.
- He instructs us to focus on our relationship with the "Lord our God" the self-Existent or Eternal God.

God's focus on the heart was not accidental, but purposefully because the heart is the most interior organ of the body. 1 Chronicles 29:9 shows the condition of the people's hearts because they gave willingly. They not only had a heart to give, but they did so with pleasure and gladness. They did not give grudgingly, but cheerfully and did not feel they were pressured to do it.

How Can We Walk Upright Before the Lord

For many, it is not impossible for man/woman to walk upright before the Lord. Perfection is made possible when we learn to walk in the spirit and not in the flesh. This characteristic of "perfection" according to scripture is one where it means to walk in and complete the race that is before us according to Hebrews 12:1-3.

We know that we all have a sinful nature, but with the help and guidance of the Holy Spirit, we can overcome most temptations that we encounter. We are also able to use the tools we are given to "fight the good fight," so as not to remain in bondage to wrongful thoughts and/ or behavior. Our focus should be on the word of God, as we "study to show ourselves approved," according to:

> *Study to shew thyself approved unto God, a workman that needeth not to be ashamed, rightly dividing the word of truth.*
>
> 2 TIMOTHY 2:15

> *Finally brethren, whatsoever things are true, whatsoever things are honest, whatsoever things are just, whatsoever things are pure, whatsoever things are lovely, whatsoever things are of good report; if there be any virtue, and if there be any praise, think on these things.*
>
> PHILIPPIANS 4:8

And likewise when our focus is on the word of God according to Philippians 4:8-9. We are able to "condition" our bodies and our minds to the point we can live the Christian virtues that will bring us closer to God.

It is the power in the word of God that will empower us to exercise self-control, and subsequently successfully win the race that will ensure our names in the Lamb's Book of Life.

16. Pure:

Who shall ascend into the hill of the Lord? Or who shall stand in his holy place: He that hath clean hands, and a pure heart; who hath not lifted up his soul unto vanity, nor sworn deceitfully. He shall receive the blessing from the Lord, and righteousness from the God of his salvation. This is the generation of them that seek him, that seek thy face, O Jacob. Selah

PSALM 24:3-6

Blessed are the pure in heart: for they shall see God.

MATTHEW 5:8

Seeing ye have purified your souls in obeying the truth through the Spirit unto unfeigned love of the brethren, see that ye love one another with a pure heart fervently.

1 PETER 1:22

The scriptures above highlight the characteristics and qualifications necessary for the type of people that will inherit the earth. Four of the requirements to inherit eternal life are:

    a.   One must have clean hands

    b.   One must have a pure heart

c. One must not be one who exalts his soul to the vanity of idols and sin

d. One must be truthful

Acceptance of Jesus Christ as Lord and Savior creates a new creature; a newness in the soul that Christians will experience as follows:

a. Purity of soul
b. Obedience to the truth
c. Yieldedness to the Holy Spirit
d. Love without hypocrisy
e. Love with fervency
f. Purity of heart
g. The new birth by the Word

Meeting those requirements will ensure the blessings and righteousness from the Lord that he has promised.

17. Single:

And they continued stedfastly in the apostles' doctrine and fellowship, and in breaking of bread, and in prayers. And fear came upon every soul: and many wonders and signs were done by the apostles. And all that believed were together, and had all things common; And sold their possessions and goods, and parted them to all men, as every man had need. And they, continuing daily with one accord in the temple, and breaking bread from house to house, did eat their meat with gladness and singleness of heart. Praising God, and having favour with all the people. And the Lord added to the church daily such as should be saved.

Acts 2:42-47

Servants, be obedient to them that are your masters according to the flesh, with fear and trembling, in singleness of your heart, as unto Christ; Not with eyeservice, as menpleasers; but as the servants of Christ doing the will of God from the heart. With good will doing service, as to the Lord, and not to men: Know that whatsoever good things any man doeth, the same shall he receive of the Lord, whether he be bond or free.

EPHESIANS 6:5-8

The temples were used to gather because of the ability to hold large gatherings sometimes amounting to thousands at one time. These types of community gatherings served provisions to those in need without charge. Many people sold their belongings perhaps except their own homes, in order to meet the needs of those that were without. These types of fellowships also served as a revival to stay abreast of the teachings and preaching's of the apostles. Because of the goodness of their hearts, the Lord added to the church on a daily basis to replenish that which was given out. Neither the church nor the people suffered hardship.

18. Soft:

For he performeth the thing that is appointed for me: and many such things are with him. Therefore am I trouble at his presence: when I consider, I am afraid of him. For God maketh my heart soft, and the Almighty troubleth me: Because I was not cut off before the darkness, neither hath he covered the darkness from my face.

JOB 23:14-17

This scripture gives us a glance at a period when Job appeared to show signs of weakness when he confessed that he was troubled because according to his understanding, God had made his heart soft. Although Job did have a fear of the Lord, and because he knew that God's ways were mysterious, he wanted to be sure he was giving in to the voice of God and not from Satan. The commentary in *The Dake Bible*,[11] it states, "After expressing confidence in God and stating that God would not use His power against him-that He would give him strength (verse 6), and that he was sure of coming out of his troubles like gold (verse 10), Job had a slight relapse into unbelief and accused God again of causing his heart to faint and be troubled (verse 16); he complained again about not being cut off while in prosperity and when he had the light of God upon him (verse 17)."

Verse 14 tells us that Job believed that his fate was predestined by God, and there was nothing he could do to change it.

Verse 15 shows Job's weakness and fragility as both faith and fear gripped him. He expressed he did not understand what God was allowing to happen.

Verse 16 indicates that Job had at last become doubtful in being assured that his relationship with God may be in trouble as his boldness waned and his heart became soft.

Although it was difficult to endure, Job still tried to maintain:

- His integrity before God
- That he was not the direct cause of this suffering
- That he would hold onto his righteousness and not let it go

19. Steadfast:

Create in me a clean heart, O God, and renew a right spirit within me.

PSALM 51:10

---

11 Dake, page 876

But the God of all grace, who hath called us unto his eternal glory by Christ Jesus after that ye have suffered a while, make you perfect, stablish, strengthen, settle you.

1 PETER 5:10

According to 1 Peter 5:10, there are four blessings that come with promise, that we are able to receive as a result of our suffering and persecution:

1. Perfections that commands us to do the following:
   a. Examine yourselves to see if you are in the true faith
   b. Prove your own selves
   c. Be perfect or put in order again
   d. Be of good comfort
   e. Be of one mind having no disputes
   f. Live in peace and harmony
   g. Be friendly and encouraging to one another
2. Establishment in the faith (Romans 1:11)
3. Spiritual strength
4. Settling or ground one in the faith

And let us not be weary in well doing: for in due season we shall reap, if we faint not.

GALATIANS 6:9

Which hope we have as an anchor of the soul, both sure and stedfast, and which entereth into that within the veil; Whither the forerunner is for us entered, even Jesus made an high priest for ever after the order of Melchisedec.

HEBREWS 6:19-20

This implies that in this newness of life (Romans 6:4) we can approach the throne of our Father in heaven full of the boldness of a son.

My heart is fixed, O God, my heart is fixed: I will sing and give praise.

PSALM 57:7

Thou will keep him in perfect peace, whose mind is stayed on thee: because he trusteth in thee.

ISAIAH 26:3

And they continued stedfastly in the apostles' doctrine and fellowship, and in breaking of bread, and in prayers. And fear came upon every soul: and many wonders and signs were done by the apostles. And all that believed were together, and had all things common; And sold their possessions and goods, and parted them to all men, as every man had need. And they, continuing daily with one accord in the temple, and breaking bread from house to house, did eat their meat with gladness and singleness of heart, Praising God, and having favour with all the people. And the Lord added to the church daily such as should be saved.

ACTS 2:42-47

Verse 42 highlights four things the early church continued steadfastly in:
- Their Apostolic teaching according to Matthew 28:20
- Their fellowship with one another according to 1 John 1:1-7
- Their practice of Holy Communion according to 1 Corinthians 10:16-17
- Consistency in prayers according to Ephesians 6:18

20. Tender:

Because thine heart was tender, and thou hast humbled thyself before the Lord, when thou heardest what I spake against this place, and against the inhabitants thereof, that they should become a desolation and a curse, and hast rent thy clothes, and wept before me; I also have heard thee, saith the Lord.

2 KINGS 22:19

This scripture addresses God's judgment on Judah at that time, and presents four reasons why Josiah would escape judgement:

a. Because his heart was tender
b. He humbled himself before Jehovah when he heard the words of the law
c. Because he rent his clothes
d. He wept before the Lord

In addition, and similar to 2 Kings 11:19, 2 Chronicles 34:27, addresses five things that bring peace with God:

a. A tender heart to comply with God
b. Self-humbling before Him
c. Hearing God's Word
d. Being in earnest about conforming to God and His Word, as suggested by the rending of clothes
e. Weeping before Him in sincerity

And be ye kind one to another, tenderhearted, forgiving one another, even as God for Christ's sake had forgiven you.

EPHESIANS 4:32

God is looking for a compassionate and sincere heart that demonstrate tenderness towards Him and others as we follow the examples of Christ.

21. Tranquil:

A sound heart is the life of the flesh: but envy the rottenness of the bones.

PROVERBS 14:30

Let's look at Webster's New World definition of the word tranquil. When speaking of people, it uses various synonyms like: calm, serene, composed, agreeable, gentle, unexcited, amicable, peaceful, measured, untroubled, sober, reasonable, even-tempered, smooth, gentle, quiet, poised, at ease, well adjusted, and patient.

The characteristics of a tranquil heart are:

- Those with a tranquil heart are quiet and strong
- Those with a tranquil heart are not affected by the adversities in life
- Those with a tranquil heart have an innate ability to deal with problems and various difficulties in life
- Those with a tranquil heart have an ultimate sense of peace
- Those with the tranquil heart professed that God is sovereign over all
- Those with a tranquil heart are confident that God always protects them
- Those with a tranquil heart find comfort in God

Proverbs 14:30 contains one of the most effective secrets to good health. Within the definition of *tranquil*, we find to possess a tranquil mind or heart, one must be free of agitation, disturbance, or turmoil, instead demonstrating a steady and stable countenance. This scripture denotes that a heart at peace gives life to the body, but one who envies will develop rottenness to the bones.

A sound or tranquil heart is free from wrath, anger, and envy. Having a tranquil heart ensures that our inner man is whole, in good health, pure and not infected with the disease of sin.

When our inner man is in a state of physical well-being, we find it easier to develop a connection in relationship with God. We are better able to resist those temptations that will allow for the influences of sin to enter our lives. That resistance also demonstrates that this is a heart that is spiritually healthy.

A heart that is strong, sound, and tranquil is strengthened daily. It can be aligned with being morally edified and restored through a regimen of daily prayer and fellowship with God.

Staying away from envy and jealousy can prevent one from participating in unpleasant and sinful thoughts and behavior like theft, slander, etc. An envious heart is decayed and will have adverse effects on your body. It's not medicine, but rather a poison that will eventually eat away from the inside out. That will promote evil which in and of itself carries the type of punishment describe in the scripture as "rottenness of the bones."

Our outward actions will show what is contained on the inside. Only the daily submission to God and our obedience to His word will give us the mental and physical strength to sustain and keep us.

22. Trembling:

And among these nations shalt thou find no ease, neither shall the sole of thy foot have rest: but the Lord shall give thee a trembling heart, and failing of eyes, and sorrow of mind: And thy life shall hang in doubt before thee; and thou shalt fear day and night, and shalt have none assurance of thy life: In the morning thou shalt say, Would God it were even! and at even thou shalt say, Would God it were morning! For the fear of thine heart wherewith thou shalt fear, and for the sight of thine eyes which thou shalt see.

DEUTERONOMY 28:65-67

Thus saith the Lord, The heaven is my throne, and the earth is my footstool: where is the house that ye build unto me? and where is the place of my rest? For all those things hath mine hand made, and all those things have been, saith the Lord: but to this man will I look, even to him that is poor and of a contrite spirit, and trembleth at my word.

ISAIAH 66:1-2

God prefers a poor man who is humble, not full of pride or puffed up more than He does the glitter of a luxurious temple. He is drawn to a godly man or woman whose afflictions and broken spirit demonstrate one who trembles at the word of God. He is looking for unwavering obedience to the commands and instructions He has set forth.

According to the *Adam Clarke Commentary*[12] this scripture speaks to the conditions under which the Israelites would have to endure for a season. "The trembling of heart may refer to their state of continual insecurity, being, under every kind of government, proscribed, and, even under the most mild, uncertain of toleration and protection; and the failing of eyes, to their vain and ever-disappointed expectation of the Messiah."

---

12 Adam Clarke

The *New International Version* reads "Among those nations you will find no repose, no resting place for the sole of your foot. There the Lord will give you an anxious mind, eyes wearing with longing, and a despairing heart."

So then, it appears in the earlier portions of Deuteronomy 28, it's clear there were going to be either blessings or curses depending on whether or not they would diligently obey the voice of the Lord and follow His commandments.

In verses 1-14, the Israelites would be overtaken by blessings if they obeyed His voice and observed His commandments. Those blessings and many more would include:

- Blessed in the city and in the country
- Blessed would they be in the fruit of their body, the produce of their ground
- Blessed shall be your basket and kneading bowl
- Blessed when they came in, and went out
- Blessed to defeat your enemies

Verse 15 introduces the curses that would come if they failed to carefully observe His commandments and His statutes. All the blessings mentioned in verse 3-14 would then befall them for their disobedience.

23. True:

Having therefore, brethren, boldness to enter into the holiest by the blood of Jesus, By a new and living way, which he hath consecrated for us, through the veil, that is to say, his flesh. And having an high priest over the house of God. Let us draw near with a true heart in full assurance of faith, having our hearts sprinkled from an evil conscience, and our bodies washed with pure water. Let us hold fast the profession of our faith without wavering; for he is faithful that promised.

HEBREWS 10:19-23

And they sent out unto him their disciples with the Herodians, saying, Master we know that thou art true, and teachest the way of God in truth, neither carest thou for any man: for thou regardest not the person of men.

MATTHEW 22:16

The New Covenant with Christ provided for all believers to walk in holy boldness in the priesthood they, through the blood of Jesus, were entitled to. The least of them that believe can now have daily access to the holiest place in heaven. All believers are striving towards the following commands:

1. Draw near to God in the manner as follows:
   - By exercising holy boldness
   - By the blood of Jesus
   - By a new and living way
   - By High Priesthood of Christ
2. Have a pure conscience
3. Have clean bodies
4. Have unwavering faith
5. Provoke others to good works
6. Be regular church attendants
7. Exhort one another daily

24. Upright:

Be glad in the Lord, and rejoice, ye righteous: and shout for joy, all ye that are upright in heart.

PSALM 32:11

O continue thy lovingkindness unto them that know thee; and thy righteousness to the upright in heart.

PSALM 36:10

The righteous shall be glad in the Lord, and shall trust him; and all the upright in heart shall glory.

PSALM 64:10

According to Psalm 32:11, those with an upright heart can expect these blessings:

- Their sins will be forgiven, covered, or atoned for
- They will not be charged with sin, and will have freedom from sin
- They will receive mercy from God, and find God to be a hiding place
- They will not be overwhelmed with sorrow
- They will be protected from trouble
- God will direct their daily path.

24. Willing

Speak unto the children of Israel, that they bring me an offering: of every man that giveth it willingly with his heart ye shall take my offering.

EXODUS 25:2

The children of Israel brought a willing offering unto the Lord, every man and woman, whose heart made them willing to bring for all manner of work, which the Lord had commanded to be made by the hand of Moses.

EXODUS 35:29

These words the Lord commanded to Moses, that he should receive from the people to accomplish the making of the tabernacle and associated materials furnishings. This command signified that the offerings already belonged to God and was only a portion of that which God had provided to them. God was specific on what offerings was to be acceptable, and only that which was willingly given. The people were instructed to give from their hearts to the building of the tabernacle to represent a renewed covenant with God; just as they previously participated in backsliding to idolatry with the willful giving of materials contributed towards building the golden calf to worship.

25. Wise:

The wise in heart will receive commandments: but a prating fool shall fall.

PROVERBS 10:8

Wise men lay up knowledge: but the mouth of the foolish is near destruction.

PROVERBS 10:14

And thou shall speak unto all that are wise hearted, whom I have filled with the spirit of wisdom, that they may make

Aaron's garments to consecrate him, that they may minister unto me in the priest's office.

EXODUS 28:3

Those that are wise tend to be more aligned with the keeping and application of the unadulterated word of God in their hearts. Another way of expressing the definition of wisdom is to exercise all of the following attributes:

- good judgment and reasoning
- clear thinking and practical knowledge
- exert carefulness and common sense
- display balance and poise
- use tact, caution, and stability

Wisdom provides one with the ability to be humble and able to receive fruitful instruction and commands from God and those in a place of legitimate authority. This type of wisdom also comes with the ability to submit without murmurings, criticisms, and complaints.

Exodus 28:3 also shows a contrast to one that shows wisdom versus one who displays a heart of foolishness; speak without consideration for truth. This person is referred to as a prating fool who is quick to speak, and leaves themselves exposed to various kinds of evil or misconduct.

PART II

CHAPTER 3

Characteristics of a Heart in Bad or Negative Condition

Note: Do synopsis or commentary on bad heart to include the state of:

Physical Heart   Mental Heart   Emotional Heart

Lending fuel to bad or negative characteristics can have a profound and even dangerous effect on the physical heart. Our mental and emotional state can be adversely impacted because of the condition(s) of our hearts. The mental state of the physical mind and body are equally important to our overall health.

To fully understand where negative characteristics, unstable mental and emotional states come from, we must understand the power of the sin that dwells within all men. According to scripture, it lies within the heart and proceeds out of the mouth and affects our actions.

> *And Jesus said, Are ye yet without understanding? Do not yet understand, that whatsoever entereth in at the mouth goeth into the belly, and is cast out into the draught? But those*

things which proceed out of the mouth come forth from the heart; and they defile the man.

For out of the heart proceed evil thoughts, murders, adulteries, fornications, thefts, false witness, blasphemies: These are the things which defile a man: but to eat with unwashen hands defileth not a man.

MATTHEW 15:16-20

So then, it is not *what* we eat, for what we eat will be cleansed from our system. It is not that we did not wash our hands *before* we ate, but rather it's what comes out of our mouths because of what we have stored in our heart.

Luke 6:45 explains it like this:

A good man out of the good treasure of his heart bringeth forth that which is good; and an evil man out of the evil treasure of his heart bringeth forth that which is evil; for of the abundance of the heart his mouth speaketh.

Good and evil are strengthened by how often that characteristic is exercised. The good treasure that Jesus speaks of comes by grace. The more men walk in sinfulness, the more they will continue in sin.

CHARACTERISTICS OF A NEGATIVE (BAD) HEART

Part 2 of this book outlines those characteristics that best describe those who ignore the commands outlined in the gospel of Jesus Christ, and those whose lives display and/or demonstrate their unwillingness to be followers of Christ, and who openly and blatantly show their disobedience to the word of God. The conditions of their heart are key factors in why they are resistant to the ordinances and commands of the word of God.

> *I am sought of them that asked not for me; I am found of them that sought me not; I said, Behold me, behold me, unto a nation that was not called by my name. I have spread out my hands all the day unto a rebellious people, which walketh in a way that was not good, after their own thoughts; A people that provoketh me to anger continually to my face, that sacrificeth in gardens, and burneth incense upon altars of brick; Which remain among the graves, and lodge in the monuments, which eat swine's flesh, and broth of abominable things is in their vessels; Which say, Stand by thyself, come not near to me, "for I am holier than thou. These are a smoke in my nose, a fire that burneth all the day. Behold, it is written before me, I will not keep silence, but will recompense, even recompense into their bosom. Your iniquities, and the iniquities of your fathers together saith the Lord, which have burned incense upon the mountains, and blasphemed me upon the hills, therefore will I measure their former work into their bosom.*
>
> ISAIAH 65:1-7

In the New Testament, Romans 10:21 sums it up even better than in the Old Testament Isiah 65:1-7 above:

> *But to Israel he saith, All day long I have stretched forth my hands unto a disobedient and gainsaying people.*
>
> ROMANS 10:21

Here God is showing how patient He was then, and even now with us. He provides the knowledge we need to bring us to repentance, and accepting His will, His word and His way. We are encouraged to not follow those whose walk was in obstinance in past days, but to heed His counsel that we might not err.

Disadvantages of negative thinking:
Downside, challenge, harm, hinder, detriment, burden.

Studies show that there is plenty of documentation that having a negative or pessimistic view of life can also produce negative results in our health as well as our overall daily living. These studies also outline that people who tend to display negative emotions are at a higher risk for heart disease because these emotions are often associated with stress which in turn can cause a higher heart rate or higher blood pressure.

People in this group who carry the burden of stress-related challenges, are also more likely to lean toward unhealthy methods for handling those challenges by choosing negative plans of action like abusing prescribed or illegal medications, binge eating, or other harmful alternatives that can cause damage to their health.

When we allow stressful attitudes and feelings become unmanageable, they then become detrimental to our overall health. Stressful situations can upset the body's hormonal balance which in turn causes the chemicals required for happiness, causes harm to the immune system. Unmanaged stress that continue on persistently can decrease our lifespan. Likewise, anger that is not managed can lead to several health conditions such as hypertension and/or digestive disorders. Harboring negative thoughts, biases, insignificant frustrations, and unforgiveness in our hearts are patterns that create an unhealthy environment.

Disadvantages:

Isaiah 14:12-15 describes some of the characteristics Satan displayed when he declared the five "I Wills" against God

> *How art thou fallen from heaven, O Lucifer; son of the morning, how art thou cut down to the ground, which didst weaken the nations. For thou hast said in thine heart, (1)* **I will ascend into heaven,** *(2)* **I will exalt my throne above the stars of God:** *(3)* **I will sit also upon the mount of the congregation, in the sides of the north:** *(4)* **I will ascend above the heights of the clouds;** *(5)* **I will be like the most High.** *Yet thou shalt be brought down to hell, to the sides of the pit.*
>
> ISAIAH 14:12-15

This scripture demonstrates the actions of Satan after he corrupted his own heart. His jealousy and envy of God caused him to take on a spirit of hubris where one places themselves on a pedestal as they exalt themselves. Hubris is defined as one who possesses an excessive amount of pride or self-confidence. One who has stored up in their heart arrogance, conceit, haughtiness, pride, and vanity. There is a difference between arrogance and hubris. Arrogance tends to be one's excessive pride relating to how they are better than others. While hubris is extremely self-belief in one's abilities, and may have nothing to do with others at all. Hubris, when cultivated, seems to turn other people into our competitors.

Several of the characteristics listed in Part 2 of this book had become embedded in the heart of Satan. He dared to think he could compete with, and or replace God on the throne; as his intent was to control the whole host of angels to stand with him, as opposed to the one-third that followed with him when he was exiled from heaven. His declaration of the "I Will's" suggests his desire to make a power play for the throne of God. This demonstrates how this characteristic did and can result in self-destruction for anyone who thinks so highly of themselves.

Types of Heart Conditions

1. Backslider:

The backslider in heart shall be filled with his own ways: and a good man shall be satisfied from himself.

PROVERBS 14:14

Let no man say when he is tempted, I am tempted of God: for God cannot be tempted with evil, neither tempteth he any man: But every man is tempted, when he is drawn away from his own lust, and enticed. Then when lust hath conceived, it bringeth forth sin: and sin, when it is finished, bringeth forth death. Do not err, my beloved brethren.

JAMES 1:13-16

Some think it is just the sinful acts that they slip back into that defines them as a backslider. However, backsliding occurs first in the heart and causes one to slowly slip away from the Lord. When one falls into a state where God's word, His holiness, and their previous devotion to God fades away, they have entered the apostate phase which is extremely dangerous. The enemy is cunning and can draw you into that place where you no longer seek the things of God; you lose your zeal to pray; worldly and carnal things soon replace the spiritual joy you once had.

> *Draw nigh to God, and he will draw nigh to you. Cleanse your hands, ye sinners, and purify your hearts, ye double-minded. Be afflicted and mourn, and weep: let your laughter be turned to mourning, and your joy to heaviness. Humble yourselves in the sight of the Lord, and he shall lift you up.*
>
> JAMES 4:8-10

To return to a place of wholeness one must go back to square one where you admit that you have fallen from grace; that you acknowledge your walk has become disorderly; and you need to repent of those sinful things that you allowed to weigh you down, pray God's forgiveness and move forward in the faith, joy and peace you once had. It is imperative that we examine ourselves periodically and repent if we find that we have allowed anything to compromise our heart and put our standing with God in jeopardy.

> *Take heed brethren, lest there be in any of you an evil heart of unbelief, in departing from the living God. But to exhort one another daily, while it is called to day; lest any of you be hardened through the deceitfulness of sin.*
>
> HEBREWS 3:12-13

It is also equally important that we fellowship with other like-minded Christian as we lift each other up daily. Saints need one another to encourage them in their walk and counsel one another to not abandon their previous profession of faith. As believers, we should advocate the purpose of remaining a part of the household of faith as we continue to assemble ourselves with our congregations.

2. Bitter or Embittered

And they shall make themselves utterly bald for thee, and gird them with sackcloth, and they shall weep for thee with bitterness of heart and bitter wailing.

EZEKIEL 27:31;

Looking diligently lest any man fail of the grace of God; lest any root of bitterness springing up trouble you, and thereby many be defiled;

HEBREWS 12:15

But if you have bitter envying and strife in your hearts, glory not; and lie not against the truth. This wisdom descendeth not from above, but is earthly, sensual, devilish. For where envying and strife is, there is confusion and every evil work.

JAMES 3:14-16

The scriptures above denote the condition of the heart when bitterness has seeped in and taken hold. One cannot possess true wisdom when one embraces bitterness. Even if there is an attempt to defend religion; that defense comes from a place of falsehood.

The *Dake Annotated Reference Bible* lists the characteristics of both false wisdom and divine wisdom.[13]

Here are eight characteristics of false wisdom:
1. Bitter envying (verses 14, 16)
2. Strife in the heart (verses 14, 16)

---

13 Dake page 458

3. Glory in profession (verse 14)
4. Earthly, having this life only in view (verse 15)
5. Sensual living only to satisfy the animal appetites (verse 15)
6. Devilish, inspired by demons (verse 15)
7. Confusion (verse 16)
8. Every evil work (verse 16)

Here are eight characteristics of divine wisdom
1. Pure – chaste holy and clean (verse 17)
2. Peaceable (verse 17, Hebrews 12:14)
3. Gentle – meek, modest, and kind (verse 17)
4. Easily entreated – not stubborn or obstinate, but yielding to others (verse 17)
5. Full of mercy – always forgiving and performing acts of kindness (verse 17)
6. Full of good fruits (Galatians 5:22-23)
7. Without partiality – having no respect of persons (verses 17, James 2:1-10)
8. Without hypocrisy – open, honest, genuine, and true (verse 17)

3. Covetous:

The definition of covetous means to have a desire for or envy of; and to demonstrate selfishness and greed.

> *But thine eyes and thine heart are not but for thy covetousness, and for to shed innocent blood, and for oppression, and for violence, to do it.*
> JEREMIAH 22:17

Eyes full of adultery, and that cannot cease from sin: beguiling unstable souls: an heart they have exercised with covetous practices; cursed children.

2 PETER 2:14

For the love of money is the root of all evil which while some coveted after, they have erred from the faith, and pierced themselves through with many sorrows.

1 TIMOTHY 6:10

References to being corrupt and unmerciful/scripture references 2 Timothy 3:1-9; Jude 4:19.

Those with this type of heart give much time to images of committing sinful acts; they spend time with thoughts and deeds of seduction of the innocent and those unaware, naive, and inexperienced.

The Ten Commandments speak to the sinfulness of those who covet:

1. **1 Timothy 6:10-12:** The love of money is the root of all evil: money in and of itself is not evil, it is necessary to take care of daily living. But we should not allow it to become something we place above everything else.
2. **Proverbs 15:27:** Do not seek or lust after material things, for a greedy person becomes a worshipper as they idolize the things of the world. Those that are greedy bring adversity upon their household.
3. **Psalm 10:2-4:** The prideful will persecute those less fortunate as they boast about the things they desire and/or covet. They are purposeful about not seeking after God and His righteousness.

4. **Deceitful:**

Then said I, Ah Lord God, behold, the prophets say unto them, Ye shall not see the sword, neither shall ye have famine; but I will give you assured peace in this place. Then the Lord said unto me, The prophets prophesy lies in my name: I sent them not, neither have I commanded them, neither spake unto them, they prophesy unto you a false vision and divination, and a thing of nought, and the deceit of their heart.

JEREMIAH 14:13-14

The heart is deceitful above all things, and desperately wicked: who can know it?

JEREMIAH 17:9

For from within, out of the heart of men, proceed evil thoughts, adulteries, fornications, murders, thiefs, covetousness, wickedness, deceit, lasciviousness, an evil eye, blasphemy, pride, foolishness: All these evil things come from within, and defile the man.

MARK 7:21-23

The answer to those scriptures above lies in Jeremiah 17:10:
I the Lord search the heart, I try the reins, even to give every man according to his ways, and according to the fruit of his doings.

Most people do not have a thorough understanding of just how deceitful their heart is, or how much that deceitful heart is the main contributor of their actions and motives. That negative attitude can be applied to those who gain their wealth by using nefarious and dishonest means and don't realize they themselves are being subject to the influence of unruly spirits that seek to deceive them also. They operate unaware that their gain is short-lived and will soon be lost without warning. They fail to understand that the only stability lies with God almighty.

According to Mark 7:21-23, here are thirteen deceitful sins of the heart that damn the soul:

1. Evil thoughts
2. Adulteries
3. Fornication
4. Murders
5. Thefts
6. Covetousness
7. Wickedness
8. Deceit
9. Lasciviousness
10. An evil eye
11. Blasphemy
12. Pride
13. Foolishness

The deceitfulness mentioned above or any mind activity that is not brought to the obedience of Christ are all works of the flesh.

5. Despiteful:

Being filled with all unrighteousness, fornication, wickedness, covetousness, maliciousness, full of envy, murder, debate, deceit, malignity, whisperers. Backbiters, haters of God, despiteful, proud, boasters, inventors of evil things, disobedient to parents. Without understanding, covenant-breakers, without naturals affection, implacable, unmerciful: Who knowing the judgment of God, that they which commit such things are worthy of death, not only do the same, but have pleasure in them that do them.

ROMANS 1:29-32

The scripture outlined above is full of characteristics unbecoming to the Christian walk. Actually, it described someone who has fallen into various states of apostasy, which is to desert their faith and backslide into sinfulness as if they had no hope. This first chapter of Romans according to *The Dake Bible* list twenty *The Dake Bible* list twenty stages[14] of apostasy:

1. They did not glorify God
2. Became unthankful
3. Vain in imaginations
4. Became dark in heart
5. Professed to be wise
6. Became fools
7. Changed God's glory
8. Dishonored their bodies
9. Changed the truth to a lie
10. Worshipped creation as God
11. Served creatures, not God
12. Submitted to vile passions
13. Women became lesbians
14. Men went into sodomy
15. Rejected knowledge of God

---

14 Dake page 304

16. Became reprobate in mind
17. Fully perverted sexually
18. Filled with iniquities
19. Despised coming judgment
20. Gloried in wickedness

6. Diabolical:

But a certain man named Ananias, with Sapphira his wife, sold a possession, And kept back part of the price, his wife also being privy to it, and brought a certain part, and laid it at the apostles' feet. But Peter said, Ananias, why hath Satan filled thine heart to lie to the Holy Ghost, and to keep back part of the price of the land?

ACTS 5:3

And supper being ended, the devil having now put into the heart of Judas Iscariot, Simon's son, to betray him;

JOHN 13:2

Then one of the twelve, called Judas Iscariot, went unto the chief priests, And said unto them What will ye give me, and I will deliver him unto you? And they covenanted with him for thirty pieces of silver. And from that time he sought opportunity to betray him.

MATTHEW 26:14-16

The term *diabolical* in and of itself gives a menacing definition according to *Merriam Webster*, which describes it as relating to or characteristic of the devil: a devilish or diabolical plot. Other comparable words are fiendish, demonic, hellish, infernal, evil, sinister, malevolent, malicious, malignant, immoral, nefarious, vicious, vile, wicked, inhuman, and savage to name a few.

This word is in direct contradiction or opposite of words that describe the antonym angelic, angelical, celestial, heavenly, godly, holy, saintly, ethical, moral, good, righteous, and virtuous.

7. Discouraged:

And wherefore discourage ye the heart of the children of Israel from going over into the land which the Lord hath given them? Thus did your fathers, when I sent them from Kadeshbarnea to see the land. For when they went up unto the valley of Eschol, and saw the land, they discouraged the heart of the children of Israel, that they should not go into the land, which the Lord had given them.

NUMBERS 32:7-9

Whither shall we go up? Our brethren have discouraged our heart, saying, The people is greater and taller than we; the cities are great and walled up to heaven; and moreover we have seen the sons of the Anakims there.

DEUTERONOMY 1:28

These words spoken because of the Lord's commandment to Moses, to send twelve men from the head of each tribe, up to search the city of Canaan that had been given to them by God. This was the land of milk and honey that had been promised by God. When the twelve spies looked over the hillside, their observation caused them to come to the following conclusions:

a. The land was as God said it would be; one that flowed with milk and honey.

b. The people appeared to be very strong.

c. The cities were protected with barricades, were walled and very strong.

d. Giants occupied the land. It was said they, the spies, were small as grasshoppers in comparison.

e. They determined, they could not go up against the people of the land, because they were stronger and bigger.

While the twelve spies acknowledged there was great potential is possessing the land; the fear of having to come up against the giants presented them with an unforeseeable victory. Hence, they brought back a negative report to the congregation, which greatly discouraged the people to the point of murmuring.

8. Double:

Of Zebulun, such as went forth to battle, expert in war, with all instruments of war, fifty thousand, which could keep rank, they were not of double heart.

1 CHRONICLES 12:33

If any of you lack wisdom, let him ask of God, that giveth to all men liberally, and upbraideth not; and it shall be given him. But let him ask in faith, nothing wavering. For he that wavereth is like a wave of the sea driven with the wind and tossed. For let not that man think that he shall receive anything of the Lord. A double-minded man is unstable in all his ways.

JAMES 1:5-8

Draw nigh to God, and he will draw high to you. Cleanse your hands, ye sinners; and purify your hearts, ye double minded. Be afflicted and mourn, and weep: let your laughter be turned to mourning, and your joy to heaviness. Humble yourselves in the sight of the Lord and he shall lift you up.

JAMES 4:8-10

Being double-minded refers to one who doubts God because they are still torn between both those things that are spiritual and those things that are carnal. God is looking for those who are willing to serve God and not mammon. Being double-minded serves one who is conflicted about making a total commitment to God.

9. Erroneous:

Ye therefore, beloved, seeing, ye know these things before, beware lest ye also being led away with the error of the wicked, fall from your own stedfastness. But grow in grace, and in the knowledge of our Lord and Savior Jesus Christ. To him be glory both now and for ever. Amen.

2 PETER 3:17

We are of God: he that knoweth God heareth us; he that is not of God heareth not us. Hereby know we the spirit of truth, and the spirit of error.

1 JOHN 4:6

We should know the difference between the Spirit of truth which is the Holy Spirit and the spirit of error which Satan. In 1 Timothy 4:1-2 we are given a snapshot of the differences between the two. *Now the Spirit speaketh expressly, that in the latter times, some shall depart from the faith, giving heed to seducing spirits, and doctrines of devils; Speaking lies in hypocrisy: having their conscience seared with a hot iron. Forbidding to marry, and commanding to abstain from meats, which God hath created to be received with thanksgiving of them which believe and know the truth.*

We can garner seven things[15] that are influenced by these spirits that promote erroneous living and practices:

1. Departing from the faith (v1)
2. Giving heed to seducing spirits (v1)
3. Giving heed to doctrines of devils (v1)
4. Speaking lies in hypocrisy (v2)
5. Having the conscience seared with a hot iron (v2)
6. Forbidding to marry (v3)
7. Commanding to abstain from meats (v3)

In 1 John 4:6 Dake references 7 ways to test false prophets[16] by:

Beloved, believe not every spirit, but try the spirits whether they are of God: because many false prophets are gone out into the world. Hereby know ye the Spirit of God: Every spirit that confesseth that Jesus Christ is come in the flesh is of God. And every spirit that confesseth not that Jesus Christ is come in the flesh is not of God: and this is that spirit of antichrist, whereof ye have heard that it should come and even now already is it in the world.

1 JOHN 4:1-3

1. Their confession of Jesus (v 2-3)
2. Their relationship with the world (v5;)
3. How they receive Christianity (v 6)

---

15 Dake page 414
16 Dake page 485

4. Their attitude toward the commandments of God (v 6)
5. Love of the brethren (v 6)
6. The indwelling Holy Spirit (v 4-6)
7. The Word of God (v 6)

10. Evil:

But this thing I commanded them, saying, Obey my voice, and I will be your God, and ye shall be my people: and walk ye in all the ways that I have commanded you, that it may be well unto you. But they hearkened not, not inclined their ear, but walked in the counsels and in the imagination of their evil heart, and went backward, and not forward.

JEREMIAH 7:24

Yet they obeyed not, not inclined their ear, but walked every one in the imagination of their evil heart: therefore I will bring upon them all the words of this covenant, which I commanded them to do; but they did them not.

JEREMIAH 11:8

And ye have done worse than your fathers; for behold, ye walk every one after the imagination of his evil heart, that they may not hearken unto: Therefore will I cast you out of this land into a land that ye know not, neither ye nor your fathers, and there shall ye serve other gods day and night, where I will not shew you favour.

JEREMIAH 16:12-13

Take heed brethren, lest there be in any of you an evil heart of unbelief. In departing from the living God. But exhort one another daily, while it is called today; lest any of you be hardened through the deceitfulness of sin.

HEBREWS 3:12

These scriptures give examples of Israel's failure to acknowledge the instructions and commands of God. They were delivered from the wilderness and given the promise of many blessings to include great fortune and success. But their sinfulness to walk backward caused them to be cut off by God from that prosperity. They forfeited that promise because they returned to their previous evil practices of unbelief; and became deceitful as they continued to walk in sin. That turning away was evidence of a hardened and evil heart that resulted in apostasy or backsliding. There are several stages that lead to apostasy or being in a backslidden state:

1. They were openly rebellious against God.
2. They refused to hear God's commands.
3. They fell into frequent sin and blatant transgressions against God's word.
4. Their hearts became hardened to the point they refused to hear God's voice.
5. They continually fell into a state of unbelief.
6. Their faith waned and they refused to come to repentance.
7. Their actions demonstrated they had withdrawn from God.

11. Foolish and darkened:

Because that, when they knew God, they glorified him not as God, neither were thankful: but became vain in their imaginations, and their foolish heart was darkened. Professing themselves to be wise, they became fools. And changed the glory of the incorruptible God into an image made like to corruptible man, and to birds, and fourfooted beasts, and creeping things.

ROMANS 1:19-23

According to an article by Dr. Steven J. Lawson titled, "No Excuse,"[17] there are several reasons why even though they knew God, and the people had no excuse for not acknowledging God:

- The people did not honor Him as God and give thanks.
- They became futile in their speculations.
- Their foolish hearts were darkened.
- They professed themselves to be wise.
- They became fools.
- They changed the glory of the incorruptible God for an image in the form of corruptible. man, and of birds and four-footed animals and crawling creatures.

As we come to the verses for this study, Paul teaches that God has made Himself known to every man (verses 19-20). However, every person has rejected this knowledge of God (verses 21-22) and replaced it with idolatrous thoughts of another god of their own making (1:23).

Part I: The Revelation of God (Romans 1:19)
Paul writes, "Because that which is known about God is evident within them; for God made it evident to them (verse 19). Paul is describing God's revelation of Himself to all people. This is what theologians call *general revelation*. To be clear, there are two different kinds of revelation

---

17 Dr. Stevens L. Lawson

by which God has made Himself known to mankind. These two categories are *general revelation* and *special revelation*.

A. General Revelation:

The first category is general revelation, which is the self-disclosure of God in a general, non-saving way. It is called general because this knowledge about God is made known to the entire human race. There is no one on planet earth, on any continent, on any island, who has not received general revelation about God. General revelation reveals the existence of God and makes known His attributes. But it does not reveal the way to know God. This knowledge of God is sufficient to condemn, but it is not sufficient to save.

At the end of verse 19, Paul further explains, "for God is evident to them." This is any important statement, because no man has ever found God on his own. God must take the initiative to reveal Himself to man. God must make the truth about Himself evident, if God is to be known, He must act first and disclose Himself to the human race.

B. Special Revelation:

This second category is special revelation, which is what we have in His written word (verses 2, 17). This is often referred to as saving revelation because it is absolutely necessary for someone to exercise faith in Jesus Christ. Special revelation is a fuller disclosure by which God reveals to mankind the way to know Him. This saving revelation is found exclusively in the written words, which alone tells us about the living Word, Lord Jesus Christ. What we know of the person of

Christ and the plan of salvation is found in the written word of God.

Paul will tell us later in Romans 10:17, "Faith comes by hearing, and hearing by the word of Christ." No one can be saved without hearing the gospel, which is found in special revelation. That is why we preach the gospel to the world. They can only come to a saving knowledge of Jesus Christ by the special revelation found in the Bible.

Part II. The Reality of God (Romans 1:20)

Paul enlarges what he has said when he writes, "For since the creation of the world His invisible attributes, His eternal power and divine nature, have been clearly seen" (verse 20). This says that God has revealed Himself to man from the beginning of the world. This divine self-disclosure started long before the New Testament times in which Paul writes. This revelation of God started before the call of Abraham and the birth of the nation of Israel. This manifestation of God started before the Tower of Babel or the flood in the days of Noah. This general revelation of God began at the creation of the world.

A. God is Omnipotent:

The apostle explains that creation itself reveals "His invisible attributes."

B. God is Eternal:

The general revelation about God's being also communicates His "eternal power." The Creator must have existed before His creation.

C. God is All-Wise:

Any look at creation also reveals that God is stunningly brilliant in His design of the universe. He is able to create with perfect wisdom that reveals His own perfections. Consider how the earth is precisely tilted on its axis at the exact angle it is, spinning at the correct rate of speed in 24-hour rotations. Think of the pinpoint accuracy in the distance of the earth from the sun. If the earth were any closer to the sun, it would burn up. If this planet was any further away, it would freeze. As the earth spins, it is perfectly exposed to the sun so that there can be the growth of plant life. This is a revelation of the perfect wisdom of God.

Consider the many rivers of the earth that flow into the vast oceans, the evaporation of water in the forming of clouds, and the moving of those clouds by the wind over the landmass. Consider the rain that ensues, the dropping of the water back onto the landmass, the way that it runs off into streams, how the streams flow into the rivers, and the rivers back into the ocean. This is nothing less than the brilliant design of God. As anyone looks at creation, he should see the sheer genius of the Creator on display.

D. Understood Through What Has Been Made

Moreover, we see the faithfulness of God in creation through the rotation of the seasons of the year, year after year. We see His unfailing faithfulness through the coming of the harvest every year. We see His consistent reliability through God providing food for the human race day after day, as we live upon the earth. We see the wrath and anger of God as we look at the hurricanes, tornadoes, and tsunamis. We see the peace of God in the calm after the storm. God has made His "divine nature" known to every single person through what He has made. To believe that all that exists merely happened by sheer chance or random fate, or that everything has created itself, is absolute nonsense.

Part III. The Rejection of God (1:21-22)
But despite this clear revelation of God, men, by and large, have rejected it. The world is not gladly receiving this truth concerning the existence and character of God. Rather than desiring more knowledge about God, the very opposite is occurring. Though God has made Himself known to all people, they have chosen to turn away from this truth and reject it. This refusal underscores what Paul wrote later regarding the total depravity of the human heart: "There is none who understands, none who seeks for God: (Romans 3:11). Because of their inherent sinful corruption, they turn away from God rather than seek Him.

A. Futile in their Speculations
When a person rejects the truth about God, it puts him in a very dangerous place. We see the result of their rejection of God as Paul continues, "They became futile in their speculations" (verse 21). That they became "futile" (mataioo) means that their thinking became "useless, worthless, vain, foolish." They conjured up in their darkened minds empty speculations about who God is. They began to have vain imaginations about God that have no basis in reality whatsoever. They began to create with their hands images of what they perceived God to be like. In doing so, these God rejectors became idolaters, who create self-conceived gods of their own insane imagination. This idol creating is the

direct result of rejecting the truth about God when it was made known to them.

Paul emphatically asserts that, "their foolish heart became darkened." This word foolish (moros) comes from the Greek word from which we derive the English word moron. He is saying that these God rejectors became moronic, incapable of having rational thoughts about God. Rejecting the light always increases the darkness. The sin of rejecting the truth about God inevitably results in a devastating effect upon anyone's thinking processes. Rejecting divine truth always short circuits man's rational abilities. Paul says their foolish heart was "darkened." Rejecting the light, their hearts became darkened. God blew out the candle and left them to grope in the dark about who He is and what He is like.

B.   Professing to be Wise

Paul succinctly states, "Professing to be wise, they became fools" (verse 22). This arrogant claim to be wise documents how self-deceived fallen mankind is. They declare them-selves to be wise, beating their own chests, and elevating themselves in their own sin-blinded eyes. They proclaim the brilliance of their own intellect, thinking they are wiser than the One who made them.

The result of this rejection of God is found in the next verse. Please note this downward spiral that descends into greater darkness from the revelation of God (verse 19-20), to the rejection of this truth about God (verse 21), to the insanity that results (verse 21b-22), to the replacement of God with idolatry (verse 23). Idolatry is not man climbing upward with higher thoughts about God. Idolatry is the total opposite. It is man spiraling down into a lower state of debased thinking and depraved living (verse 24-32).

C. The Terrible Exchange

The inevitable consequence of rejecting the truth about God is devastating. Paul writes that they "exchanged the glory of the incorruptible God for an image in the form of corruptible man and of birds and four-footed animals and crawling creatures" (verse 23). This replacement of the glory of God for the grossness of the creature is a destructive exchange. This trade is giving up treasures of truth diamonds for the trash of lies.

They trade the knowledge of the ever living God for pieces of wood and metal that are crafted into image of a man. They then bowed down before these man-crafted images and worshiped what their own hands produced.

D. The Downward Spiral

In verse 24, Paul will announce that God will give these idolaters over into judgment. According to the doctrine of total depravity, men are running away from the knowledge of God in their ignorance. Their fingers are in their ears, lest they hear the truth about God. They cover their eyes, lest they see something.

The human race has started at the high point of receiving the knowledge of God, but then adamantly rejected it. They then exchanged the knowledge of God for their own hand made idols.

E. How Shall We Then Live?

What are the implications of the truth we have examined in these verses? What does this passage say about our responsibility to God? What do these verses require of us? What positive application can there be from such negative statements?

F. Give Glory to God

First, we must be careful to do the very opposite of what we see describes in these verses. Paul relates, "They did not honor Him as God or give thanks "(verse 21). We must be those who give glory to God. We must be worshipers of God. We must bow down before this one true God and come to Him through His Son, the Lord Jesus Christ.

G. Give Thanks to God

Second, we must be giving thanks to God in everything. If unbelievers withhold the giving of thanks to God, we must be those who give Him thanks for what He has down for us and what He is to us. We must give thanks to all things both big and small. We must give thanks for His provision to us, for His protection to us, for His care, for His providence in our lives, for His Son, for grace, for salvation.

H. Bear Witness to God

Third, we must be actively involved in telling others about the truth of God. We must be bearing witness of the gospel to those who are in need of the saving knowledge of God. This involves being willing to go on short term missions. It involves encouraging those who are actively engaged in doing what they can to spread the gospel of Jesus Christ. This requires us to do all that we can to be involved in reaching people with the gospel of Jesus Christ.

12. Fretting:

The foolishness of man perverteth his way: and his heart fretteth against the Lord.

PROVERBS 19:3

Fret not thyself because of evil men, neither be thou envious at the wicked; For they shall be no reward to the evil man: the candle of the wicked shall be put out.

PROVERBS 24:19-20

Fret not thyself because of evildoers, neither be thou envious against the workers of iniquity. For they shall soon be cut down like the grass, and wither as the green herb. Trust in the Lord and do good: so shalt thou dwell in the land, and verily thou shall be fed. Delight thyself also in the Lord, and he shall give thee the desires of thine heart. Commit thy way unto the Lord: trust also in him, and he shall bring it to pass. And he shall bring forth thy righteousness as the light, and thy judgment as the noonday. Rest in the Lord, and wait patiently for him: fret not thyself because of him who prospereth in his way, because of the man who bringeth wicked devices to pass. Cease from anger, and forsake wrath: fret not thyself in any wise to do evil.

PSALM 37:1-8

The scripture in this Psalm gives a clear command to those who feel they are worried or in a critical state of distress.

Scripture promises us that the prosperity of the wicked man is only temporary and those that engage in evil will receive punishment that will be eternal. Therefore, for us to envy or fret goes against what God has commanded us and is in vain. There are seventeen commands that come out of Psalm 37 that instructs us against being vexed, which is to allow ourselves to become heated or immersed in being annoyed, frustrated, or worried.

1. Fret not because of evildoers (verse 1)
2. Do not be envious of evil workers
3. Trust in the Lord (verses 3, 5)
4. Do good (verses 3, 27)
5. Delight yourself in the Lord (verse 4)
6. Commit your way unto the Lord (verse 5)
7. Rest in the Lord (verse 7)
8. Wait patiently for God (verses 7, 34)
9. Fret not because of prosperity of others
10. Fret not because of wicked plots against you
11. Cease from anger (verse 8)
12. Forsake wrath
13. Fret not yourself to do evil
14. Depart from evil (verse 27)
15. Keep His way (verse 34)
16. Mark the perfect man (verse 37)
17. Behold the upright

Examples of people who fretted against God:

Adam

> *And the man said, The woman whom thou gavest to be with*
> *me, she gave me of the tree, and I did eat.*
>
> GENESIS 3:12

Adam quickly placed blame on the wife God gave him, as if he would not have sinned if God had not given him Eve. Placing blame on others is a trait of the natural man and not the spiritual man. This scripture also proves that Adam was present and aware of when Eve was tempted but did not put forth the effort to protect both him and her of the warning God had previously given to not eat of the tree. Adam was not forced to eat but chose to eat of the tree as well and did so.

Cain

> *And Cain said unto the Lord, My punishment is greater than*
> *I can bear. Behold, thou hast driven me out this day from the*
> *face of the earth; and from thy face shall I be hid; and I shall*
> *be a fugitive and a vagabond in the earth; and it shall come to*
> *pass, that every one that findeth me shall slay me.*
>
> GENESIS 4:13-14

This scripture shows the anguish Cain was in when he cried out to the Lord, after he was cursed for slaying his brother, Abel. He fretted over having to confront what he thought was unjust punishment for his murderous deed, which was to be sentenced to work the ground even harder than before. He was also sentenced to becoming a "fugitive" and a "vagabond" in the earth.

13. **Froward or Perverse:**

They that are of a forward heart are abomination to the Lord: but such as are upright in their way are his delight. Though hand join in hand the wicked shall not be unpunished: but the seed of the righteous shall be delivered.

PROVERBS 11:20

A man shall be commended according to his wisdom, but he that is of a perverse heart shall be despised.

PROVERBS 12:8

He that hath a froward heart findeth no good: and he that hath a perverse tongue falleth into mischief.

PROVERBS 17:20

An article from "Let God be True"[18] outlines the characteristics of a froward heart and perverse tongue. "A bad heart or bad speech brings trouble. Both will curse you twice. If you allow evil in your heart, you will not find good coming your way in life. If you allow your tongue to say evil things, you will fall into mischief because of it. Here is a sober warning of certain consequences for not ruling your spirit and speech. Beware!

- A man with a froward heart is rebellious - he despises obeying his father, pastors, employers, or the government. He is arrogant and will excuse his sins every time. He can hurt those around him without any remorse. He is seldom happy or content no matter the efforts taken to please him.

18 Let God be True

- A man with a froward heart does not find good. He is not blessed. He will not know the favor of God or men in his life. He is doomed to trouble, no matter how hard he seeks God, because his heart is evil to God and men.
- A perverse tongue is corrupt, froward, obstinate, unreasonable, wicked, and wrong. To consider its opposite, a wholesome tongue is pure, gentle, gracious, correct, reasonable, kind, righteous, and right. A perverse tongue says the wrong things at the wrong time in the wrong way. Such speech is hurtful, irritating, disruptive, and destructive.
- A man with a perverse tongue cut those near him, especially his family. He criticizes anyone he wishes, whenever he pleases. He ridicules authority. He prays in church and curses on the way home. He flatters his enemies and yet rips his tender wife within the hour. He slanders, back bites, and whispers about others without thought. He is negative and complaining. His tongue is perverse. He cannot say holy kind things except in hypocrisy.

God hates this bitter fountain, which sprays venom from a poisoned well. Such a man will fall into mischief. He will be troubled, for God and men will oppose him. Any friend he has are not true friends, for they are only there for what they can get. He wonders why bad things happen to him, but he cannot admit his speech is corrupt.

The truth of the matter is that a froward heart produces a perverse tongue. It is near impossible to have one without the other, because out of the abundance of the heart the mouth speaks (Matthews 12:33-37). Therefore, an evil heart will bring corrupt speech, which brings the double curse of this proverb. Keep thy heart with all diligence (Proverbs 4:23).

Having a froward heart and perverse tongue shows you are not guarding the thoughts of your heart or the words of your tongue as you should. Your sins of the heart and evil speech have bought God's judgment and man's disapproval upon your life. Repent! Turn your heart and lips to righteousness.

14. Hard:

If there be among you a poor man of one of thy brethren within any of thy gates in thy land which the Lord thy God giveth thee, thou shalt not harden thine heart, nor shut thine hand from thy poor brother: But thou shalt open thine hand wide unto him, and shalt surely lend him sufficient for his need, in that which he wanteth.

DEUTERONOMY 15:7-8

To harden the heart and show a lack of compassion against someone in need was guaranteed to result in having your own blessings from God cut off.

Harden not your heart, as in the provocation, and as in the day of temptation in the wilderness: When your fathers tempted me, proved me, and saw my work.

PSALM 95:8-9

Harden not your hearts, as in the provocation, in the day of temptation in the wilderness. When our fathers tempted me, proved me, and saw my works forty years.

HEBREWS 3:8

These scriptures give commands for Christians to come to the aid and give relief to a poor brother:

1. If your brother suffers hardships that causes him to become poor, we should not shut our hands or hardened our hearts against him.
2. We should be generous in our giving to ensure our brothers needs are met.
3. We are cautioned to stand up to our responsibility as brethren, and not purposely perpetrate a reason to avoid rending help.
4. God is looking for us to give freely and unselfishly without harboring feelings of regret and/or grief because it is the right thing to do.
5. We should always stand ready to help those who are poor and less fortunate than ourselves because there will always be those who are in need.

This also cautioned the Israelites to cease from provoking God lest they be excluded from the promises he had given. Here, God also gives a challenge to try Him, or test Him to see if His word was kept.

15. Haughty:

The rich man's wealth is his strong city and as an high wall in his own conceit. Before destruction the heart of man is haughty, and before honour is humility.

PROVERBS 18:11-12

Pride goeth before destruction, and an haughty spirit before a fall.

PROVERBS 16:18

Those who carry their riches as a banner and display a high-minded attitude are cautioned about being enclosed within their own sense of arrogance, narcissism, self-admiration, and pride. To harbor haughtiness within the heart will lead one to look down on their neighbors with scorn and as being worthless and beneath them. But sooner or later, these types will be brought low and humble, and their spirits will soon suffer heartache, suffering and destruction.

A modern-day example of one who demonstrated a prideful and haughty heart was the arrogance of the owners of the Titanic. As it churned along the iceberg-filled water of the North Atlantic on April 15, 1912, at top speed, the captain ignored warnings by other ships of the dangers that lie ahead. Approximately 1500 lives were lost as the historical "unsinkable" ship sunk in less than three hours.

A few biblical examples of those who suffered destruction through pride are:

> *Thine heart was lifted up because of thy beauty, thou hast corrupted thy wisdom by reason of thy brightness: I will cast thee to the ground, I will lay thee before kings, that they may behold thee.*

> EZEKIEL 28:17

Lucifer

Satan's obsession with his beauty and his perfect state led him to become proud and corrupt. He was so impressed with his own beauty, wisdom, and power that he began to seek for himself the honor and glory that belonged to God the creator. That type of sinfulness was self-generated in pride and corruption which resulted in his punishment of being exiled from heaven.

> *And when Jehu was come to Jezreel, Jezebel heard of it; and she painted her face, and tired her head, and looked out a window.*

And as Jehu entered in at the gate, she said Had Zimri peace, who slew his master? And he lifted up his face to the window, and said Who is on my side? Who? And there looked out to him two or three eunuchs. And he said, Throw her down. So they threw her down and some of her blood was sprinkled on the wall, and on the horses: and he trode her under foot. And when he was come in, he did eat and drink, and said, Go, see now this cursed woman, and bury her: for she is a king's daughter. And they went to bury her, but they found no more of her than her skull, and the feet, and the palms of her hand.

2 KINGS 9:30-33

Jezebel

The story of Jezebel, the wife of King Ahab, is set with one of the most intriguing women of the Bible. Although she is described as a vixen, strong-willed, courageous, and politically savvy; she brings with her a history of treachery, conspiracy, and bloodshed. Her downfall was due to the heavy influence she carried in spreading apostasy within the Jewish nation of Israel by her practice of worshipping Baal, the pagan god of fertility, along with her efforts to bring paganism and idolatry to the people.

Moab

We have head of the pride of Moab; he is very proud, even of his haughtiness, and his pride, and his wrath: but his lies shall not be so.

ISAIAH 16:6

Moab was a son of Lot, who was a nephew of the Israelite patriarch, Abraham. The Moabites belonged to the same ethnic stock as the

Israelites. Moab was exiled to Babylon for his arrogance and idolatry. That exile was also due to the Moabites gross ingratitude even though Abraham had saved Lot from Sodom. They were also punished for their maltreatment of the children of Israel and for engaging Balaam to curse the children of Israel while they journeyed in the wilderness.

According to Isaiah, Moab was so proud and was well-known to be so haughty that he would "reject" this counsel. He would neither send the usual tribute to the land of Judea (Isaiah 16:1), thus acknowledging his dependence on them; nor would he give protection to the exiled Jews as they should wander through his land, and thus try to conciliate their favor, and secure their friendship. In Isaiah 44:25, Moab was known for the boasting of his strength and security and did not feel he needed the friendship of the Jews.

Jeremiah 48:28-29 speaks on the pride of Moab

> *O ye that dwell in Moab, leave the cities and dwell in the rock, and be like the dove that makeh her nest in the sides of the hole's mouth. We have heard the pride of Moab, (he is exceeding proud) his loftiness and his arrogance, and his pride, and the haughtiness of his heart.*

16. Heavy:

> *As he that taketh away a garment in cold weather, and as vinegar upon nitre, so is he that singeth songs to an heavy heart.*
>
> PROVERBS 25:20

> *Strong drink unto him that is ready to perish, and wine unto those that be of heavy hearts.*
>
> PROVERBS 31:6

A person with a heavy heart is not in a mood to have anyone try to cheer him up by telling jokes, singing songs, offering comical stories, or making comments are that unimportant at the time. As a matter of fact, these approaches do not cheer anybody up, but they may find it insulting, and counterproductive. So then instead of helping that person get warm, it's like you take away the little bit of protection they had, which leaves them worse off than they were.

When people are facing traumatic events, or seem to be in a place where there seems to be no way out, or no light at the end of the tunnel, then no matter what type of cheerfulness you try to give them they remain fearful and worried.

Often when we try to have a conversation with people who are grieving or suffering, they feel like their pain or whatever it is they're going through means nothing to us. To them, our approach is foolishness as we ramble on and on as if we don't understand what they're going through. They will forget whatever it is we said to them the minute we leave the room. Even though we were trying to cheer them up, a person with a heavy heart will take that as you are being immature, insensitive, and downright rude in their time of need. So then, instead of them appreciating your presence, they can't wait for you to leave.

A show of Christian love and caring should involve a sense of compassion and understanding of whatever it is they are going through. When we try to administer empathy or sympathy, we show we care about the circumstances they are going through. The best support for a person with a heavy heart is to try and take upon yourself some of the grief they are experiencing.

17. Idolatrous:

But godliness with contentment is great gain. For we brought nothing into this world, and it is certain we can carry nothing out. And having food and raiment let us be therewith content. But they that will be rich fall into temptation and a snare, and into many foolish and hurtful lusts, which drown men in destruction and perdition. For the love of money is the root of all evil, which while some coveted after, they have erred from the faith, and pierced themselves through with many sorrows.

1 TIMOTHY 6:9

Love not the world, neither the things that are in the world. If any man love the world, the love of the Father is not in him. For all that is in the world, the lust of the flesh, and the lust of the eye, and the pride of life, is not of the Father but is of the world. And the world passeth away, and the lust thereof: but he that doeth the will of God abideth forever.

1 JOHN 2:15-16

Now the works of the flesh are manifest, which are these: Adultery, fornication, uncleanness, lasciviousness. Idolatry, witchcraft, hatred, variance, emulations, wrath, strife, seditions, heresies. Envying, murders, drunkenness, reveling, and such like: of the which I tell you before, as I have also told you in time past, that they which do such things shall not inherit the kingdom of God.

GALATIANS 5:19-21

On an article from The Biblical Counseling Coalition on the subject of The Idolatrous Heart,[19] it states: "The heart of idolatry is truly central to most of the issues we face in counseling. Just like the other sins with

---

19 Biblical Counseling Coalition

which we struggle, idolatry is rooted in the immaterial part of man we refer to as the heart. The heart contains your thoughts, beliefs, desires, mind, will, and emotions. That is why the heart can be referred to as the control center of your being. The heart of mankind is deceitful and wicked according to Jeremiah 17:9, and the sinful nature that we battle feeds the wicked desires of the heart.

This article cites the New Living Translation (NLT) of that scripture which reads as follows:

> *When you follow the desires of your sinful nature, your lives will produce these evil results: sexual immorality, impure thoughts, eagerness for lustful pleasure, idolatry, participation in demonic activities, hostility, quarreling, jealousy, outbursts of anger, selfish ambition, divisions, the feeling that everyone is wrong expect those in your own little group.*

Each of us struggles with the horrendous sin of idolatry on a daily basis. As Galatians 5 tells us, idolatry is a desire of our sinful nature. It is reflected in our choices, our words, our use of time, what or who we spend our money on, and where we spend it. In our culture, we tend to think of idolatry as an eastern religious system such as Buddhism or Hinduism, or as pagan worship of the trees and animals. But the truth is, idolatry is not only bowing down to statues, it is anything that means more to you than God does. It is manifested when getting what you want has become more important than what God desires for you. Simply put, anything that you are loving, desiring, or serving more than God is an idol of the heart.

We are constantly being tempted to sin in this manner. While many technological advances exist in the world, including new things to idolize and worship, Satan uses the same tricks and methods to bait the trap that he has employed since the Garden of Eden when the big lie and the great temptation was initiated by Satan when he said, "You will be like God."

Man has wanted to be his own god since that time. Being your own god means freedom from accountability. They succumbed to the lust of the eyes, the lust of the flesh, and the pride of life. Sin and guilt entered the world, and to this day Satan uses the same tactics against us."

The NLT version of the scripture Titus 2:12-13 gives instructions on how to correct the idolatrous heart:

> *And we are instructed to turn from godless living and sinful pleasures. We should live in this evil world with self-control, right conduct, and devotion to God, while we look forward to that wonderful event when the glory of our Great God and Savior, Jesus Christ will be revealed.*
>
> TITUS 2:12-13

> *Wherefore, my dearly beloved, flee from idolatry*
>
> 1 CORINTHIANS 10:14 (NKJV)

> *Dear children, keep away from anything that might take God's place in your hearts.*
>
> 1 JOHN 5:21 (NLT)

If this is truly your desire, confess it to Him in prayer and then follow up your prayer with actions that will demonstrate the fruit of your repentance. Try the following actions:

- Begin to admit the sin of idolatry exists in your heart. Admission is the first step but removing the idols in your hearts and life is an ongoing process. If you have struggled with idolatry for a long time, you have habits that are deeply ingrained. You will find yourself admitting and confessing this sin frequently, but do not be discouraged! Recognize that God is working to clean out the deception in your heart.

- Identify exactly what you want that you are not getting. Some examples would be feeling better or having a better day.
- Identify if your desire is biblical and be able to support it with scripture (in context). This is important because emotions can lead us to justify our desire for certain things. Yet feelings provide unreliable as a method of living life to glorify Godd.
- Place your desires and wants on the altar of sacrifice to God.

God wants to change the way you think, which will change the way you live. Reject the thoughts of what you want and desire for each day. Begin to obey God by fulfilling the "One Another" commands in Scripture. Take your focus off yourself, begin to live for Christ and serve your family, church, or friends.

18. Impenitent:

But after thy hardness and impenitent heart treasurest up unto thyself wrath against the day of wrath and revelation of the righteous judgment of God; Who will render to every man according to his deeds.

ROMAN 2:5

The New International Version of this scripture reads:

But because of your stubbornness and your unrepentant heart, you are storing up wrath against yourself for the day of God's wrath, when his righteous judgment will be revealed.

An article by Nicholas Bizic, dated August 19, 2015[20] explains 3 Bible tips on impenitence:

1. Impenitent means unrepentant or hard-hearted.
2. One must sincerely repent of his sins in order to be forgiven.

    Repent therefore and be converted, that your sins may be blotted out, so that times of refreshing may come from the presence of the Lord.

    ACTS 3:19

3. God desires everyone to come to repentance. Ask for His help to deeply repent.

    The Lord is not slack concerning His promise, as some count slackness, but is longsuffering towards us, not willing that any should perish but that all should come to repentance.

    2 PETER 3:9

The reference of "hardness" in Romans 2:5 is an indication that those that reject the knowledge of God's mercy must have some type of heart problem. The Greek word *hardness* is a word from which we get the English medical terminology "sclerosis". That implies there is a hardening of something related to the physical heart. That stubbornness, or hardened, or obstinate attitude towards God shows there is a spiritual disconnect or sclerosis type condition of the heart.

The wrath that man will face is clearly said here, in the sense that, since any man who chooses to demonstrate willful ignorance when revelation has been provided, is then deserving of the kind of wrath

---

20 Nicholas Bizic

that God will apply. Anyone who walks away from the word of God acknowledges, they hear or know the truth, but resists it and choses to continue to walk in an unrepentant state.

> *Therefore say unto the House of Israel, thus saith the Lord God; repent and turn yourselves from your idols; and turn away your face from all your abominations.*
>
> EZEKIEL 14:6

In the above verse, God wanted His people to be cleansed from the sin of idolatry, in their thoughts and their actions. God wants each of us to have a true sense of guilt and sinfulness. After getting that understanding, we should know that God's mercy is available through Christ Jesus. The evidence of repentance is seen when we persistently strive to live a life that honors God by walking in obedience with Him and surrendering our lives to His will. True repentance requires a sincere turning away from sin which will result in a change of action.

19. Mischievous:

> *Happy is the man that feareth always: but he that hardeneth his heart shall fall into mischief.*
>
> PROVERBS 28:14

> *Be not thou envious against evil men, neither desire to be with them. For their heart studieth destruction, and their lips talk of mischief.*
>
> PROVERBS 24:1-2

> *An heart that deviseth wicked imaginations, feet that be swift in running to mischief.*
>
> PROVERBS 6:18

They conceive mischief, and bring forth iniquity. Their heart prepares deceit.

JOB 15:35

As for both these kings, their hearts shall be to do mischief, and they shall speak at one table: but it shall not prosper; for yet the end shall be at the time.

DANIEL 11:27

In Proverbs 6:18, it describes the type of mischief that is carried out in the heart. And scripturally, the heart has been identified as the source of all good or evil. Because God searches the heart, He looks to see how, when and where those mischievous thought will be put into action. That scripture also points to "feet" that will be swift in doing that.

A mischievous person traffics in the following:
- Deliberately plans to be evil
- Use hasty and spur-of-the moment efforts to carry out evil plans
- Exercising a heart that devises wicked imaginations
- Uses nefarious methods to exact revenge on those they despise

Proverbs 24:1-2 encourages us not to envy wicked men or look to them for friendship. Even though we will often be tempted to covet the things that appear to make them look prosperous; God knows there is a very good reason why we should not envy them. Those that are wicked often display other characteristics used to deceive others while their character is perverse, obstinate, and contrary. Their goal and intentions are to deceive and lead others astray of God's word and the blessing He has in store for them.

This Proverb encourages us to:
- Be wise and not be influenced by big homes and fancy cars
- Not be swayed by designer brands and fast cash
- Not be drawn by seeing them enjoy extravagant vacations
- Not be jealous of their connects to the rich and famous

While on the surface all those things may seem to offer value, if ill-gotten, they will only bring destruction and headache. Mischievous people love living sinful lives that is contrary to the word and will of God.

Job 15:35 also gives contrasting characteristics of those with a mischievous heart. While they appear to be both elegant and impressive, their hearts are full of these types of mischievous seeds that Satan sows in their hearts:
- Fraud and deception
- Lust which in turn brings forth sin, then death
- Live to formulate and then execute evil plans

20. Obstinate:

But Sihon king of Heshbon would not let us pass by him: for the Lord thy God hardened his spirit, and made his heart obstinate, that he might deliver him into thy hand, as appeareth this day.

DEUTERONOMY 2:30

This scripture speaks to the opposition Moses faced as he led the Israelites through yet another city as they journeyed on to Canaan. They encountered Sihon, king of Heshbon who did not want them to pass through. Even with promises to not disturb anyone or offers to pay for any inconveniences the king demonstrated strong-minded, stubborn, and obstinate persistence in not letting them pass. But God knew there would be great resistance from Sihon, and warned Moses that war with them would be necessary.

Let's look at Webster's definition of the word "obstinate": stubborn, firm, headstrong, opinionated, **strong-minded**, callous, resistant, **unwavering**, **unbending**, **unyielding**, are just a few ways to describe this word. To be clear, some of those words could be used in either a positive or negative sense depending on the context or intended purpose. Exodus 32:9-10 gives another variation or use of the word obstinate and that is *stiffnecked. And the Lord said unto Moses, I have seen this people, and, behold, it is a stiffnecked people.: Now therefore let me alone, that my wrath may wax hot against them, and that I may consume them: and I will make of thee a great nation.*

> *Be strong and of a good courage: for unto this people shalt thou divide for an inheritance the land, which I sware unto their fathers to give them. Only be thou strong and very courageous, that thou mayest observe to do according to all the law, which Moses my servant commanded thee: turn not from it to the right hand or to the left, that thou mayest prosper whithersoever thou goest. This book of the law shall not depart out of thy mouth; but thou shall meditate therein day and night, that thou mayest observe to do according to all that is written therein: for then thou shalt make thy way prosperous, and then thou shall have good success. Have not I commanded thee Be strong and of a good courage; be not afraid neither be thou dismayed: for the Lord thy God is with thee whithersoever thou goest.*
>
> JOSHUA 1:6:9

In this passage, Joshua is told to be strong and of a good courage. In other words, to be strong-willed, unwavering, unbending, or unyielding. In the context of this scripture, God is giving six commands to be obedient:

1. Be strong and of good courage which is repeated again in (verse 6, 7 and 9)
2. Observe to do all the law (verse 7)
3. Turn not from it to the right hand or to the left
4. This book of the law shall not depart out of your mouth, but you shall meditate in it day and night (verse 8)
5. Be not afraid (verse 9)
6. Neither be dismayed

The benefits for this obedience are:

1. That thou may prosper wherever you go (verse 7)
2. That you may make your way prosperous (verse 8)
3. You shall have good success
4. God will be with you wherever you go (verse 9)

However, as with Sihon king of Heshbon, in verse 26-30, he refused to grant permission to Moses and the Israelites to pass through his territories which were east of the river Arnon as Moses had been commanded by God. But God hardened Sihon's spirit and he rejected Moses' request to pass through. Because of his hardened heart, Sihon's use of those characteristics of being **unyielding**, **strong-willed**, **obstinate** put him at odds with God's command to Moses and a war ensued where God allowed Moses and the Israelites to possess the land. To be clear, it was Sihon's determination, resistance and prejudice against the Israelites that caused God to hardened his spirit. Moses offered a peaceful transition and Sihon resisted.

So, we see two different circumstances where leaders exerted a form of courage or strength. But depending on how it is used may or may not be in one's best interest.

21. Overcharged:

And take heed to yourselves, lest at any time your heart be overcharged, with surfeiting, and drunkenness and cares of this life, and so that day come upon you unaware. For as a snare shall it come on all them that dwell on the face of the whole earth.

LUKE 21:34-35

But know this, that if the goodman of the house had known in what watch the thief would come, he would have watched' and would not have suffered his house to be broken up. Therefore be ye also ready: for in such an hour as ye think not the Son of man cometh.

MATTHEW 24:43-44

Definition of overcharged: to overburden, strain, overtaxed, exaggerate, overdraw, overload, too full or too heavy.

We often find ourselves in a place where we have failed to take heed to the commands we have been given; and soon after, discover we have allowed ourselves to be overtaken with a feeling of sickness after over indulgence in the things of life. If we're not careful, we will allow a spirit of heaviness or worry to burden us to the point we are not in a mental state to make sound decisions. So then, we want to be in a mental and spiritual state that will insure we are prepared in the day of the Second Coming and won't be caught off guard or unaware.

22. Proud:

*By thy great wisdom and by thy traffick hast thou increased
thy riches, and thine heart is lifted up because of thy riches:*

EZEKIEL 28:5

*The Lord shall cut off all flattering lips, and the tongue that
speaketh proud things: Who have aid, With our tongue will
we prevail; our lips are our own: who is lord over us?*

PSALM 12:3

*Whoso privily slandereth his neighbor, him will I cut off: him
that hath an high look and a proud heart will not I suffer.*

PSALM 101:5

These scriptures speak to the importance of words, for they can
either reward, damn or condemn. A proud heart can cause one to walk
in arrogance, insolence and with a haughty attitude. As if their presence
and purpose is of the utmost importance and should be recognized as
one who demands privilege, immediate gratification and often sees
others as being beneath them or less than.

Most everyone desires to be successful, comfortable, stress free and
have a feeling of being established in life. Sometime, throughout our
lifetime, we look forward to having a prosperous future. But we
recognize also that life can bring many changes. There is very little that
is guaranteed or totally secured or constant.

A principle of life shows us that godly men can establish a secure
future that is deep-rooted for their family. And, while it appears that
wicked living yields some short-lived or material gains, it will only last for
a short period of time, because God will not allow the wicked to prosper.

According to Psalm 12:3, those who walk in proudness are easily recognized because they display these characteristics:

- They are dishonest
- They are boastful and brag about their status
- They display arrogant attitudes
- They are smooth talkers but give lying compliments to deceive others
- They peddle falsehoods

Psalm 101:5 shows the judgment that God will take upon those who vilify his neighbor by:

- Spreading false reports
- Brings false charges or accusations against them
- Slanders them in any way

For those who think highly of themselves, and tend to look down at others with contempt, God does not look favorably upon. God will not reward those with that type of character to find a seat in the house of God as a faithful minister.

23. Sorrowful

Even in laughter the heart is sorrowful: and the end of that mirth is heaviness.

PROVERBS 14:13

This verse expresses what those that are stressed and burdened with a heavy heart are experiencing. Being in a state of sorrow can leave the heart so heavy that some may feel compelled to put on a smile and feign happiness to mask how they really feel. Laughter is often used to cover up the heartache of feeling empty or try to deceive with a display that all is well.

Those who make jokes, pretend to be the life of the party, or partake of substances that alter the mood do so with a heavy heart to hide the realities of life.

> *A merry heart maketh a cheerful countenance: but by sorrow of the heart the spirit is broken.*
>
> PROVERBS 15:13

When you display a sense of happiness, it shows on the outside appearance for all to see. This type of presentation is in direct contrast with one who carries a heavy heart full of sorrow. That kind of heaviness can cause the spirit to be broken.

A sorrowful or troubled heart should seek God for comfort that only a relationship with Him can give. Without that personal relationship, false pretenses and foolish laughter will continue to be unhappy and disillusioned.

24. Stubborn

> *Thou art wearied in the greatness of thy way; yet saidst thou not, There is no hope thou hast found the life of thine hand; therefore thou wast not grieved.*
>
> ISAIAH 57:10

> *Search the scriptures, for in them ye think ye have eternal life: and they are they which testify of me. And ye will not come to me, that ye might have life.*
>
> JOHN 6:30-40

In these scriptures, we're given a more than adequate description of what a stubborn heart looks like.

The negative indications show up when you:

- Refuse to acknowledge there is a problem, like in having various types of addictions where you continue with your own method of treatment for whatever the trials and tribulation that seem to be unsurmountable challenges are. For example, those fighting alcoholism seek justification through partaking because the alcohol itself represses the trauma of that challenge.
- Husband/wives who encounter the challenges that come with family life like raising children or working to satisfy the financial obligations that goes with keeping the household together. The "stubborn heart" will blame their partner for being stressed and miserable, then seek comfort and relief outside their marriage with someone else, thus leading them down the road to the sins of adultery and fornication.
- This type of heart not only operates in those with addictions, but in anyone (as John 5:39-40) indicates that even though you search the scriptures, you still refuse to walk in the truth after hearing the truth.
- The stubborn heart is the one that keeps you far away from God and does not operate in your favor. The stubborn heart presents itself as spiritual deception, it is the obstacle that stands in the way of finding your way to God.
- This type of heart keeps truths and facts hidden deep, not allowing those truths and facts to surface where you can see and understand why someone would want to continue to suffer through tormented situations repeatedly.

The solution to those and many other stubborn ways are just a prayer away. We can ask God to soften our stubborn hearts; turn away from those sinful acts that keep us distracted from hearing God's answer.

> *And the Father himself, which hath sent me, hath borne witness of me. Ye have neither heard his voice at any time, nor seen his shape. And ye have not his word abiding in you: for whom he hath sent, him ye believe not. Search the scripture; for in them ye think ye have eternal life: and they are they which testify of me. And ye will not come to me, that ye might have life. I receive not honour from men. But I know you, that ye have not the love of God in you.*
>
> JOHN 5:37-42

This scripture addresses the difference between faith and belief. There are those who refuse to believe and cannot be convinced, regardless of what evidence is presented (John 5:40). Jesus was critical of the local religious leaders for never hearing the voice of God. They are rejecting Jesus and His message (John 5:18) because they are unwilling, not because they are uniformed. Scripture never asks anyone to show "blind faith", which is belief without evidence.

God does not offer "proof" to all people: it won't necessarily produce obedience or trust. Knowing that God exists does not mean obedience will follow (James 2:19). Having information and/or knowledge does not always mean trusting in God, as Israel's own disobedience showed. In fact, while the Pharisees were knowledgeable in the scriptures, it did not mean they were willing to accept Jesus (John 7:17).

25. Subtle: (Subtil)

> *And, behold, there met him a woman with the attire of an harlot, and subtil of heart.*
>
> PROVERBS 7:10

While all of Chapter 7 seems to suggest that it may serve only as a warning to be vigilant regarding the lust of the flesh; and it does to great extent, however, it's clear after further research that anyone can possess a subtil heart. We'll explore several ways this negative characteristic can be present in one's disposition.

The Dake Annotated Reference Bible[21] outlines 10 points about how this defines a harlot as follows:

1. Their attire or marks that advertise them for hire (v.10; Gen. 38)
2. Their subtlety of heart (v. 10 and 11)
3. Their boisterous and loud disposition
4. Their gadabout disposition (v. 11-12)
5. Their stubbornness and persistence in pursuing innocent victims (v. 11). They have no respect for the good of men, married or unmarried, innocent, or guilty of immoral crimes. They gloat over causing young men to fall into sin and husbands to go astray.
6. They are bold, unashamed, impudent, and unlawfully familiar (v. 13)
7. They are flatterers (v.5, 14-21)
8. They are deceitful of heart (v. 13-21)
9. They are liars (v. 14-21)
10. They are temptresses and seducers (v. 21)

The *King James Version Dictionary* describes the word variations of "subtil" as:

---

21 Dake

A. Subtil:

1. Thin, not dense or gross; as *subtil* air; *subtil* vapor; a *subtil* medium
2. Nice; fine; delicate
3. Acute; piercing; as *subtil* pain.
4. Sly; artful; cunning; crafty; insinuating; as a *subtil* person, a *subtil* adversary.
5. Planned by art; deceitful; as a *subtil* scheme.
6. Deceitful; treacherous.
7. Refined; fine; acute; as a *subtil* argument.

B. Subtility:

1. Fineness

C. Subtilization (from subtilize)

1. The act of making subtil, fine or thin. In the laboratory, the operation of making so volatile as to rise in steam or vapor.
2. Refinement; extreme acuteness.

Webster's New World Roget's Thesaurus[22] defines subtil (subtle) as being:

Misleading, illusive, mentally suggestive, precise, complex, exact, detailed.

The range that this chapter covers tends to warn us all of the subtleties that exist with the art of deception. All should be concerned with the engagement with possessing our vessel in sanctification, in a respectful manner, with dignity and not get caught up in some of the lustful traps that await us. When we let our guard down or allow

---

22 Webster's

ourselves to frequent places or participate in activities that add to the various temptations the world has to offer, we can all be misled.

One of the main reasons we are to guard our hearts is to keep us from the snares of Satan. We must control our own bodies and passions to avoid the serious and disastrous consequences. But if we are to keep God's commands, we will surely avoid the self-ruins that awaits those that transgress. Our awareness of those sins that tend to be "more pleasant" to our flesh, also tend to leave us most exposed because they deceive our hearts, which in turn leaves us more vulnerable against being remorseful. Without having regret in our hearts after a transgression, we lose the ability to truly repent and move forward.

26. Troubled:

Let not your heart be troubled, ye believe in God, believe also in me. In my Father's house are many mansions: if it were not so, I would have told you. I go to prepare a place for you. And if I go and prepare for you; I will come again, and receive you unto myself; that where I am, there ye may be also. And whither I go ye know, and the way ye know.

Peace I leave with you, my peace I give unto you; not as the world giveth , give I unto you. Let not your heart be troubled, neither let it be afraid.

JOHN 14:1-4, 27

The verses above outlines God's promises to us that He is coming back for us at the appointed time. This promise will be fulfilled to all those who are true believers. According to scripture, Jesus Christ is coming back for the His bride, which is for all those who have given their life to Jesus and made Him their Lord and Savior. At that time, we will be given new glorified bodies, and will go to live with Him forever.

This scripture is often read to comfort those who have lost loved one to death. It is not only a scripture of comfort, but also one of hope and promise. After Jesus responds to the apprehension of His disciples by saying, "Do not let your hearts be troubled. Believe in God, believe also in me", Jesus is giving them the assurance that He is not leaving them forever, but is returning to His Father. And that where He is going, He will prepare a place for them to join Him later and dwell with Him and the Father.

This is a powerful scripture as it is meant to enlighten those whose hope seems to dwindle when they have lost a loved one. During the season of grief and mourning, the words of Jesus are often forgotten and overlooked at the joy of where our saved loved ones are and where we also may be at the appointed time. So then, there is no need for our heart to be troubled or perplexed because as believers, we do have hope in an expected end.

27. Turned Away:

But if thine heart turn away, so that thou will not hear, but shalt be drawn away, and worship other gods, and serve them; I denounce unto you this day, that ye shall surely perish, and that ye shall not prolong your days upon the land, whither thou passeth over Jordan to go to possess it.

DEUTERONOMY 30:17

For it is impossible for those who were once enlightened, and have tasted of the heavenly gift, and were made partakers of the Holy Ghost. And have tasted the good word of God, and the powers of the world to come. If they shall fall away, to renew them again unto repentance; seeing they crucify to themselves the Son of God afresh, and put him to an open shame.

HEBREWS 6:4-6

All we like sheep have gone astray; we have turned every one to his own way: and the Lord hath laid on him the iniquity of us all.

ISAIAH 53:6

But there are some of you that believe not. For Jesus knew from the beginning who they were that believed not, and who should betray him. And he said, Therefore said I unto you, that no man can come unto me, except it were given unto him of my Father. From that time many of his disciples went back, and walked no more with him.

JOHN 6:64-69

An example of one whose heart turned away from God is that of King Solomon. Despite his accumulation of great wisdom, his astute insight, and education, he slowly turned away from God. His wealth brought him many things, but it could not buy a faithful heart that would give in to the commands of God. Because we are all free moral agents, we have the choice of using the gifts God gives us or not. 1 Kings 11:1-25 gives a detail analysis of how Solomon's love of women and his gravitating toward the idolatry those women surrounded themselves with, was the cause of his fall.

For it came to pass, when Solomon was old that his wives turned away his heart after other gods: and his heart was not perfect with the Lord His God, as was the heart of David his father.

1KINGS 11:4

These were the steps in Solomon's fall:

- **Wealth:** King Solomon amassed an extraordinary amount of wealth through (1) commerce and trading; (2) gifts; (3) tribute money and (4) heavy taxation.
- **Weapons**
- **Women:** He had 700 wives, princesses, and 300 concubines
- **Turning his heart from Jehovah:** He gave in to the pressure and influences of his wives who practiced idolatry.
- **Outright idolatry:** He became a victim of the practices of the women who surrounded him.

Unfortunately, Solomon turned away from God "when he was old" according to scripture, although he died before he reached the age of 60. Turning away from God's commands will never result in gaining greater peace and/or happiness. Rather it will result in frustration and daily problems that will rob us of the peaceful life God intends for us to have.

28. Uncircumcised:

In that ye have brought into my sanctuary strangers, uncircumcised in heart, and uncircumcised in flesh, to be in my sanctuary, to pollute it, even my house, when ye offer my bread; the fat and the blood, and they have broken my covenant because of all your abominations.

EZEKIEL 44:7

Behold, the days come, saith the Lord that I will punish all them which are circumcised with the uncircumcised. Egypt, and Judah, and Edom, and the children of Ammon, and Moab and all that are in the utmost corners, that dwell in the wilderness: for all these nations are uncircumcised, and all the house of Israel are uncircumcised in the heart.

JEREMIAH 9:25-26

Verses 25–26 refer to the nations of Israel and Gentile that are to be judged and subsequently punished together.

Ye stiffnecked and uncircumcised in heart and ears, ye do always resist the Holy Ghost, as your fathers did, so do ye.

ACTS 7:51

The scriptures are speaking to those that were then, and over time have remained hardheaded, stubborn, unyielding, and unrelenting in their effort to accept the commands of God.

29. Unsearchable:
The heaven for height, and the earth for depth, and the heart of kings is unsearchable.

PROVERBS 25:3

This scripture gives a seemingly complex, yet simple comparison to the difficulty of the efforts it takes to understand the heart of someone. It addresses three things that seemingly cannot be measured; easily understood, explored, or scrutinized.

First, no one can accurately measure the heavens for its height. Regardless of having access to the most powerful instruments to research the universe, the heavens are unsearchable.

Second, no one can accurately assess the depths of the earth. No matter how often the oceans have been explored to expose new species of underwater creatures; or what theories have been considered using the most recent studies, there has not been a true measure for how deep the earth is from top to bottom.

Third, no man knows with any certainty, exactly what the heart of a king contains, because it is unsearchable.

> *I exhort therefore, that, first of all supplications, prayers, intercessions, and giving of thanks, be made for all men; For kings, and for all that are in authority, that we may lead a quiet and peaceable life in all godliness and honesty. For this is good and acceptable in the sight of God our Saviour.*
>
> 1 TIMOTHY 2:1-3

> *They search out iniquities; they accomplish a diligent search: both the inward thought of every one of them, and the heart is deep.*
>
> PSALM 64:6

The hearts of kings, presidents, and those in leadership or authority contain information that the average person knows nothing about. Their closest advisors may or may not have access or insight into what they may be thinking at one point, but not always. So, certainly persons in these leadership roles would have information that those of us at the "local" level would rarely be exposed to. These leaders, when making decisions do not have to seek advice or approval from lay persons before going forth with policies, rules and/or regulation that may impact

those whose lives may be affected. Nor do they have to give reason for their decisions.

Why are we instructed to pray for those in authority? Because they too, as all humanity, are subject to have a sinful nature, desperately wicked, and apt to fail, fall or make decisions that are not in the best interest of the people, but rather a decision that only serves their own best interest.

1 Timothy 2:1 outlines four duties of all Christians:
1. Supplications – to make humbly or earnestly known that there is a need to be met
2. Prayers – a solemn or sincere request to God
3. Intercessions – to intercede on behalf of someone else
4. Giving of thanks – express gratitude or show appreciation

Prayers are essential for our leaders that they make godly decision that will be a blessing to the people the nation or organization(s) they have rule over.

30. Whorish:

Yet will I leave a remnant, that ye may have some that shall escape the sword among the nations, when ye shall be scattered through the countries. And they that escape of you shall remember me among the nations which they shall be carried captives, because I am broken with their whorish heart, which hath departed from me, and with their eyes, which go a whoring after their idols: and they shall lothe themselves for the evils which they have committed in all their abomination. And they shall know that I am the Lord, and that I have not said in vain that I would do this evil unto them.

EZEKIEL 6:9-10

My people ask counsel at their stocks, and their staff declareth unto them: for the spirit of whoredoms hath caused them to err, and they have gone a whoring from under their God.

Rejoice not, O Israel, for joy, as other people: for thou hast gone a whoring from thy God, thou hast loved a reward upon every cornfloor.

HOSEA 4:12, 9:1

These scripture speaks to the practice of idol worshipping that would cause them to be cut off from the favor of God. Because of their whorish ways, the prophet Hosea prophesied they would suffer these twenty-one afflictions:

1. Their crops would fail.
2. Ephraim would trust in Egypt for help but would not receive it; but would be defeated and taken captive to Assyria.
3. They would not be allowed to offer wine offering to the Lord.
4. They would not be pleasing to the Lord.
5. Their sacrifices would be to them as bread for mourners who refuse to eat.
6. They would be destroyed.
7. Egypt will gather them up and bury them.
8. Nettles will be in their reassure houses, and thorns in their homes.

9. Israel will know the time of his visitation and the days of her recompense.
10. God will remember and visit the iniquity of the prophets.
11. The glory of Ephraim will fly away like a bird.
12. Israel will be cut off in conception, in the womb, and in birth.
13. I will destroy their children.
14. There will not be a man left.
15. I will depart from Israel.
16. Ephraim will bring forth children to be murdered.
17. I will drive them out of My house because of their sins.
18. I will love them no more (meaning that generation, and others should they continue in the same sins).
19. They will bear no fruit, yet if they do have children, I will slay them.
20. God will cast them away.
21. They will be wanderers among the nations.

31. Wicked:

Let favour be shewed to the wicked; yet will he not learn righteousness: in the land of uprightness will he deal unjustly, and will not behold the majesty of the Lord.

Lord, when thy hand is lifted up, thy will not see: but they shall see, and be ashamed for their envy at the people; yea, the fire of thine enemies shall devour them.

ISAIAH 26:10-11

Frowardness is in his heart, he deviseth mischief continually; he soweth discord.

> *An heart that deviseth wicked imaginations, feet that be swift in running to mischief.*
>
> PROVERBS 6:14, 18

> *Though hand join in hand the wicked shall not be unpunished: but the seed of the righteous shall be delivered .*
>
> PROVERBS 11:21

In Jeremiah 4:14-18, God commanded Judah to wash themselves of their wickedness so that they might be saved.

In the scriptures above, there are 3 characteristics that describe the wicked:

a. He will not learn righteousness when favor is from Him

b. He will deal unjustly with neighbors

c. He will refuse to recognize God in all His merciful dealings with him.

This know also, that in the last days perilous times shall come. For men shall be lovers of their own selves, covetous, boasters, proud, blasphemers, disobedient to parents, unthankful unholy, Without natural affection, trucebreakers, false accusers, incontinent, fierce, despisers of those that are good, Traitors, heady, highminded, lovers of pleasures more than lovers of God.

2 TIMOTHY 3:1-4

In this passage of scripture, there are thirty characteristics of wicked men outlined as follows:

1. Lovers of themselves, fond of oneself, selfish.
2. Covetous, fond of money.

3. Boasters, braggarts, self-exalted.
4. Proud, self-esteem, important.
5. Blasphemers.
6. Disobedient to parents, head-strong children.
7. Unthankful, ungrateful.
8. Unholy, without piety; no reverence.
9. Without natural affection: Living in unnatural affection sins; perverts; homosexuals; sodomites.
10. Trucebreakers.
11. False accusers, slanderer; adversary.
12. Incontinent, no control of appetites and passions.
13. Fierce: wild, savage; uncivilized.
14. Despisers of good men, unfriendly to good men.
15. Traitors: betrayers.
16. Heady: hasty; reckless, headstrong.
17. High-minded: senseless, conceited, silly.
18. Lovers of pleasure: sensual gratification is their god.
19. Having a form of godliness: their religion is only in their creed and formal confession of faith, not in their hearts.
20. Denying the power of godliness: Destitute of godliness, having no faith that one can be godly to this life. From such turn away.
21. Use their show of piety to gain entrance into homes to deceive.
22. Capture for their own pleasure silly (foolish) women whom they deceive.
23. Ever learning fallacies but never the knowledge of the truth.
24. Resist truth.

25. Have corrupt minds.
26. Reprobate concerning faith.
27. They are evil.
28. They seduce women – entice them to surrender chastity.
29. They increase in evil.
30. They deceive and are themselves deceived.

CHAPTER 4

Why the Condition
of the Heart Matters

THE DEFINITIONS FOR the characteristics for both a good or positive heart; or a bad or negative heart are important to determining why the condition(s) of the heart matters. There has been much focus on our emotional state, our physiological processes, and our physical health because they are weaved so closely together. Before we can expect a change in the condition of our overall health, we must consider the prospect of implementing a change in our behavior. The question becomes: How do we accomplish that?

Because God searches the heart, He knows that alone, there is little that we can accomplish, but with God all things are possible - Matthew 19:26.

As mentioned previously, we must examine ourselves, take a deep look at our actions, the thoughts we harbor or allow to influence us, and answer to question: What condition is my physical heart really in; and what do I need to do to ensure my spiritual heart is positioned where God can reach me?

There are ways to prevent some of the negative effects our behavior has on our physical heart health by implementing the following:

Examine yourself and those you associate with:
- Examine your living conditions
- Get better exercise
- Practice good sleeping habits
- Eat well balance meals
- Drinking enough water

Ways to improve the positive effects our behavior can have on our spiritual heart health by implementing the following:

Examine yourself and those you associate with:

> *Ye shall know them by their fruits. Do men gather grapes of thorns, or figs of thistles? Even so every good tree bringeth forth good fruit; but a corrupt tree bringeth forth evil fruit. A good tree cannot bring forth evil fruit, neither can a corrupt tree bring forth good fruit. Every tree that bringeth not forth good fruit is hewn down, and cast into the fire.*
>
> MATTHEW 7:16-20

> *Let this mind be in you, which was also in Christ Jesus.*
>
> PHILIPPIANS 2:5

> *I beseech you therefore, brethren, by the mercies of God, that ye present your bodies a living sacrifice, holy, acceptable unto God, which is your reasonable service. And be not conformed to this world: but be ye transformed by the renewing of your mind, that ye may prove what is that good, and acceptable, and perfect, will of God.*
>
> ROMANS 12:1-2

Be careful for nothing; but in every thing by prayer and supplication with thanksgiving let your requests be made known unto God. And the peace of God, which passeth all understanding, shall keep your hearts and minds through Christ Jesus. Finally, brethren, whatsoever things are true, whatsoever things are honest, whatsoever things are just, whatsoever things are pure, whatsoever things are lovely, whatsoever things are of good report; if there be any virtue, and if there be any praise, on these things.

PHILIPPIANS 4:6-8

Before my conclusion, I would like to also mention a formula from a biblical principle that represents a classic example of how to choose God, even in the face of adversity, or having exposure to the negative circumstances he had from his father and grandfather. To support this premise, I would like to introduce Josiah, who, according to scripture was the youngest to be king of Judah. An article from GotQuestions .org[23] shows that regardless of his tainted background, Josiah demonstrated his heart was focused on keeping the statutes and commandments of God.

"Josiah was the king of Judah from approximately 640 to 609 B.C. His reign in Jerusalem is discussed in 2 Kings 22–23 and 2 Chronicles 34–35. Josiah was the son of King Amon and the grandson of King Manasseh—both of them wicked kings of Judah. Yet Josiah was a godly king and known as one of the world's youngest kings; he began his reign at age 8 after his father was assassinated. A highlight of Josiah's reign was his rediscovery of the Law of the Lord.

---

23 GotQuestions.org

2 Kings 22:2 introduces Josiah by saying, "And he did what was right in the eyes of the LORD and walked in all the way of David his father, and he did not turn aside to the right or to the left." In the eighteenth year of his reign, he raised money to repair the temple, and during the repairs the high priest Hilkiah found the Book of the Law. When Hilkiah read it to Josiah, the king tore his clothes, a sign of mourning and repentance (verse 11).

King Josiah called for a time of national repentance. The Law was read to the people of the land, and a covenant made between the people and the Lord: "The king stood by the pillar and made a covenant before the LORD, to walk after the LORD and to keep his commandments and his testimonies and his statutes with all his heart and all his soul, to perform the words of this covenant that were written in this book. And all the people joined in the covenant" (2 Kings 23:3).

Many reforms followed. The temple was cleansed from all objects of pagan worship, and the idolatrous high places in the land were demolished. Josiah restored the observance of the Passover (2 Kings 23:2–23) and removed mediums and witches from the land. 2 Kings 23:25 records, "Before him there was no king like him, who turned to the LORD with all his heart and with all his soul and with all his might, according to all the Law of Moses, nor did any like him arise after him." God's wrath would later come upon Judah due to the evil King Manasseh had done (2 Kings 23:25), but the judgment was delayed because of Josiah's godly life and leadership (2 Kings 22:20).

Josiah died in battle versus the Egyptian Pharaoh, Necho, at Megiddo. King Josiah was buried in Jerusalem in his own tomb, and his son, Jehoahaz, took the role of king.

Much can be learned from Josiah's life that is positive:

First, Josiah shows the influence a person can have from a very young age. Even children have enormous potential to live for God and to have great impact.

Second, Josiah lived a life fully committed and obedient to God and was blessed for it.

Third, Josiah properly responded to God's word. By the time he became king, the Scriptures had long been neglected, and Josiah's heart was smitten by the failure of his people to honor God's word. Josiah had Scripture read to the people and made a commitment to live by it. "'Because your heart was responsive and you humbled yourself before the Lord when you heard what I have spoken . . . I also have heard you,' declares the Lord" (2 Kings 22:19)."

> *And the king stood by a pillar, and made a covenant before the Lord, to walk after the Lord, and to keep his commandments to his testimonies and his statutes with all their heart and all their soul, to perform the words of this covenant that were written in this book. And all the people stood to the covenant. And the king commanded Hilkiah the high priest, and the priests of the second order, and the keepers of the door, to bring forth out of the temple of the Lord all the vessels that were made for Baal, and for the grove, and for all the host of heaven: and he burned them without Jerusalem in the fields of Kidron, and carried the ashes of them unto Bethel.*
>
> 2 KINGS 23:3-4

> *Josiah was eight years old when he began to reign, and he reigned in Jerusalem one and thirty years. And he did that which was right in the sight of the Lord, and walked in the*

ways of David his father, and declined neither to the right hand, not to the left. For in the eighth year of his reign, while he was yet young, he began to seek after the God of David his father: and in the twelfth year he began to purge Judah and Jerusalem from the high places, and the groves, and the carved images, and the molten images.

2 CHRONICLES 34:1-3

2 Chronicles 34 gives a list of those things Josiah accomplished during his reign as follows:

1. Walked in the ways of David (verse 2)
2. Turned not to the right or left in following good
3. Sought God in his youth (verse 3)
4. Began as a youth to purge Judah and Jerusalem from the high places and groves, the carved images and molten
5. Broke down the altars of Baal (verse 4)
6. Cut down the images that were high above the altars of Baal
7. Cut down the groves
8. Cut down the carved images
9. Broke the molten images
10. Made dust of all the images and scattered it on the graves of them that had sacrificed to these gods
11. Burnt the bones of the priests upon their altars (verse 5)
12. Cleansed Judah and Jerusalem
13. Cleansed all the cities of the 10 tribes that were left after the destruction of Samaria (verse 6)
14. Repaired the house of God (verse 8-17)
15. Rent his clothes when he heard the reading of the newly found law of Moses (verse 19)

16. Commanded that inquiry be made of Jehovah concerning the book of the law of Moses (verse 21)
17. Recognized the cause of the wrath of God upon Israel by hearing the law read
18. Humbled himself before God (verse 27)
19. Wept before Jehovah when he heard the truth of the law of Moses
20. Gathered the elders of Israel to Jerusalem and read the law to all the people (verse 30)
21. Made a covenant before the Lord to walk after Him; to keep His commandments, testimonies, and statutes with all his heart and soul; and to perform all the words of the law of Moses (verse 31)
22. Caused all the people to agree to this covenant with God (verse 32)
23. Took away all the abominations out of all countries that pertained to Israel (verse 33)
24. Made all Israel to serve the Lord God
25. Kept the Passover at the proper time and in the correct way (verses 35:1-19)
26. Set priests in their charges (verse 35:2)
27. Encouraged them to serve Jehovah in their courses (verses 35:3-16)
28. Gave thousands of animals to the people for sacrifices (verse 35:7)

According to 2 Kings 23:5-25, he also went on to destroy and/or remove the following pagan practices:

- The Sodomite houses
- Places of idolatry

- The fire worship of Molech
- Removed sun worship and its dedicated horses and chariots
- Destroyed idolatrous altars and other idol gods
- Destroyed Jeroboam's altar and high place of Bethel
- Destroyed high places in all Samaria and kills the idolatrous priests
- He restored the Passover
- Destroyed all traffic with demons and household gods

This shows not only King Josiah's dedication, but also the extreme reformations he committed to in his personal life, and to those he felt responsible for, in order to demonstrate how serious he was to ensure God's commands were kept.

God searches and knows all hearts:
Prior to the summarized review, let's take a look at some of the most important Bible verses that address what God says about the heart.

> *But the Lord said unto Samuel, Look not on his countenance, or on the height of his stature; because I have refused him: for the Lord seeth not as men seeth; for man looketh on the outward appearance, but the Lord looketh on the heart.*
>
> 1 SAMUEL 16:7

> *And thou, Solomon my son, know thou the God of thy father, and serve him with a perfect heart and with a willing mind: the Lord searcheth all hearts, and understandeth all the imagination of the thoughts: if thou seek him, he will be found of thee; but if thou forsake him, he will cast thee off forever.*
>
> 1 CHRONICLES 28:9

The heart is deceitful above all things, and desperately wicked: who can know it? I the Lord search the heart, I try the reins, even to give every man according to his ways, and according to the fruit of his doing.

JEREMIAH 17:9-10

And the Spirit of the Lord fell upon me; and said unto me, Speak; Thus saith the Lord: Thus have ye said. O house of Israel: for I know the things that come into your mind, every one of them.

EZEKIEL 11:5

And he said unto them, Ye are they which justify yourselves before men, but God knoweth your hearts: for that is highly esteemed among men is abomination in the sight of God.

LUKE 16:15

And he that searcheth the hearts knoweth what is the mind of the Spirit because he maketh intercession for the saints according to the will of God.

ROMANS 8:27

For the word of God is quick, and powerful, and sharper than any twoedge sword, piercing even to the dividing asunder of soul and spirit, and of the joints and marrow, and is a discerner of the thoughts and intent of the heart.

HEBREWS 4:12

Summary

UNDERSTANDING WHAT THE word *brokenhearted* means in Hebrew and Greek turns it into a whole different meaning than what we're used to. We tend to think a broken heart means that someone hurt us emotionally.

However, that's only a glimpse of the picture the Bible paints. The heart (as described in Hebrew and Greek) is the entire inner being of a man.

Everything that person does it rests in their heart.

In other words, it would be what we call "the soul" in English. An entire man's personality is found in the heart. All his thoughts, emotions, intentions, and actions flow out of the heart.

It's no wonder that God must give us a new heart when we become born again. That's the only thing He has to change, and everything else will be changed with it.

Everything that a man can be broken or completely shattered. Someone's purpose, will, and desires can be stolen from them, leaving them with hopelessness and despair. The next time you deal with someone with a broken heart, remember that they cannot 'just get over it.' The Bible says God heals the brokenhearted. It's spiritual brokenness, and it must be dealt with as such. Changing our behavior requires changing our thought process, which will change our outlook or view, thinking more spiritual than carnal. That change requires a commitment to align ourselves with the true and living God through Christ Jesus.

There is a simple mathematical formula that one scripture gives to help guarantee our security in Christ and in getting our hearts right before the Lord.

> *And besides this, giving all diligence, add to the faith virtue; and to virtue knowledge; And to knowledge temperance; and to temperance patience; and to patience godliness; And to godliness brotherly kindness; and to brotherly kindness charity. For if these things be in you, and abound, they make you that ye shall neither be barren nor unfruitful in the knowledge of our Lord Jesus Christ.*
>
> 2 PETER 1:5-8

This formula can be condensed into the seven steps in spiritual math that leads to Christian virtues:

1. Add to faith virtue
2. Add to virtue knowledge (verse 5)
3. Add to knowledge temperance (Galatians 5:22)
4. Add to temperance patience
5. Add to patience godliness (1 Timothy 3:16)
6. Add to godliness brotherly kindness
7. Add to brotherly kindness love (1 Corinthians 13:4)

According to Scripture, those are the virtues that Christians should demonstrate to angels and men. The effort necessary to fulfill these seven virtues is sacrifice.

On July 13, 2022, my pastors, Dr. Fred L. and Linda G Hodge.[24] during their regular Training Camp Bible Study, spoke on the "Power of Sacrifice".

1. The depth of my love is always determined by my sacrifice.
2. Men may not recognize my sacrifice, but it never goes unnoticed by God.
3. If I am short-sighted, I will perceive sacrifices as being negatives.
4. I will succeed to the degree I am willing to abandon excuses, overcome fears and make sacrifices.
5. Anything of value that is to be obtained and maintained requires sacrifice.
6. Sacrifice puts in now and receives back later.
7. Sacrifice is the key to the door of prosperity and success.
8. The strength of any covenant is determined by the sacrifices of the partners.
9. What I give to God sacrificially He multiplies back to me in a greater measure.
10. You will succeed in life to the degree you are willing to sacrifice for your success.
11. If you sacrifice today, you will have sufficiency tomorrow.
12. Sacrifice is distasteful to the flesh.
13. Sacrifice can be personal but doesn't have to be painful.
14. For every success, there is a price to be paid and sacrifice writes the check.

---

24 Fred & Linda Hodge

So, sacrifice is the effort we put forth to build, strengthen and instill good characteristics within our hearts. Conversely, we also sacrifice when we desire to diminish those unfavorable or bad characteristics that cause our hearts to be corrupted. What will you choose?

We can see the contrast of the characteristics of the hearts of those in Part I and those in Part II. Those contrasts lays out the ground work for each of us to determine the conditions of our hearts that is best suited for a fruitful life.

> *Let no corrupt communication proceed out of your mouth, but that which is good to the use of edifying, that it may minister grace unto the hearers. And grieve not the Holy Spirit of God, whereby ye are sealed unto the day of redemption. Let all bitterness, and wrath, and anger, and clamour, and evil speaking, be put away from you, with all malice. And be ye kind one to another, tenderhearted, forgiving one another, even as God for Christ's sake hath forgiven you.*
>
> EPHESIANS 4:29-32

The following Psalm also outlines the character of God's people:

> *Who shall ascend into the hill of the Lord? or who shall stand in his holy place? He that hath clean hands, and a pure heart, who hath not lifted up his soul unto vanity, nor sworn deceitfully. He shall receive the blessings from the Lord, and righteousness from the God of his salvation. This is the generation of them that seek him, that seek thy face O Jacob. Selah.*
>
> PSALM 24:3-6

This summary ends with a reflection on the scripture above that ends with the term "selah." Some offered their interpretation of "selah" has agreed that there are some words in the Bible that we don't fully understand. However, we know that it carries significance in that we should "pause and reflect" on the specific words that precede it. That is not to say the words followed by selah are more important than any other scriptures in the Bible. But instead, they are meaningful commands and instructions that, if followed, can significantly impact our health, happiness, and relationship with Jesus Christ.

Reflection
Sow a thought, reap a habit,
Sow a habit, reap a character,
Sow a character, reap a destiny
What character does destiny say your fruit will bring? Selah

About the Author

DR. PHYLLIS GLASS is an ordained minister at Living Praise Christian Church for the Mature Adult Ministry in Palmdale, California. She has conducted workshops and seminars for work and church for more than twenty-five years. Dr. Glass is filled with the Holy Ghost and speaks and teaches under the anointing of God. Dr. Glass is the author of four books, including *God Searches the Heart*. Prior to becoming an author, she retired after ten years with the California State Department of Correction as a Credentialed Business Occupations Instructor; and twenty-three years of administration and business management in the aerospace sector. Dr. Glass holds a Doctor of Divinity degree and a Bachelor of Science degree in Business Administration. She is the mother of five adult children, two sons, three daughters, four grandsons, five granddaughters, and four great-grandchildren. Dr. Glass resides in Palmdale, California.

Bibliography

1. Dr. Greg E. Viehman,
2. Kristina Robb-Davis, How Negative Emotions Affect Health, June 12, 2020
3. Misfit Ministries, December 25, 2019, on Brokenhearted in both Hebrew and Greek
4. Dake Annotated Reference Bible, Page 282 on Circumcision of the Heart
5. Elizabeth Peale Allen, August 22, 2014
6. Stephanie Englehart, https://www.christianity.com/wiki /Christian-life/how-can-we-embrace-a-contrite-heart-and-spirit .html
7. Mark D Roberts, The Stability of Your Times
8. Dake Annotated Reference Bible, Psalm 34:4, page 928
9. Ron Edmondson, https://www.biblestudytools.com/blogs/ron -edmondson/10-reasons-david-is-called-a-man-after-god-s-own -heart.html
10. Bible.org,
11. Dake Annotated Reference Bible, Page 876

12. Clarke, Adam. "Commentary on Deuteronomy 28:65". "The Adam Clarke Commentary". https://www.studylight.org /commentaries/acc/deuteronomy-28.html. 1832.
13. Dake, page 458, False Wisdom and Divine Wisdom
14. Dake Annotated Reference Bible, Page 304, 20 Stages of Apostasy
15. Dake Annotated Reference Bible, Page 414, 7 Things that influence erroneous living
16. Dake Annotated Reference Bible, Page 485, 7 Ways to Test False Prophets
17. Dr. Steven L. Lawson, No Excuse, February 23, 2017
18. Let God Be True
19. Biblical Counseling Coalition The Idolatrous Heart
20. Nicholas Bizic, https://www.ucg.org/beyond-today/blogs/3-bible -tips-impenitence
21. Dake Annotated Reference Bible, Page 1070, 10 Points
22. Webster Dictionary
23. https://www.gotquestions.org/Josiah-in-the-Bible.html
24. Dr. Fred L. Hodge, Jr. and Linda G. Hodge, Training Camp, July 13, 2022, Living Praise Christian Church, Palmdale & North Hollywood, CA

Glossary

This list is a combination of biblical and/or dictionary definition of these terms

Backslider or Backslidden
Biblical: Implies moving away from Christ; going the wrong way spiritually; reverted to old ways; dropping out of church, losing fervor for the Lord, walking away from a ministry.

Dictionary: To lapse morally or in the practice of religion; to revert to a worse condition
Bankrupt, delinquent, derelict, incorrigible, rogue, reprobate, villain.

Bitter or Embittered
Biblical: Synonymous with resentment and envy; Cain became consumed by bitterness for his brother Abel and God, because he felt he was treated unfairly and inferior because his brother seemed to be more prosperous.

Dictionary: Having a sharp, pungent taste or smell, not sweet; often disagreeable, distasteful or distressing to the mind, accompanied by severe pain or suffering. Marked by cynicism and rancor.

Broken or Contrite

Biblical: Being so crushed by the sin and darkness of the world that we recognize there is no place to turn but to God. This kind of brokenness is an inward feeling – or having a contrite spirit over our own sinfulness which in turn leads to a combination of humility, surrender, and repentance. People who are broken and unrepentant can in turn crush other people. Being contrite causes one to be filled with a sense of guilt and the desire for atonement, penitent, to be humbled.

Dictionary: Broken: having been fractures or damaged; no longer in one piece or in working order; a person giving up all hope or one who is in despair. Contrite: feeling or showing regret for bad behavior, remorseful.

Circumcised

Biblical: The Old Testament defines a covenant between God and all Jewish Males; but is not a requirement in the New Testament. Rather Christians are encouraged to be "circumcised of the heart" by trusting in Jesus Christ and his sacrifice on the cross.

Dictionary: To perform a medical procedure of male or female genitals as a religious rite; or to purify spiritually.

Clean

Biblical: A clean or pure heart will produce words and pure actions. Just as one cannot get salt water out of a fresh water spring, or fresh water out of the ocean; so too we cannot get righteousness out of a wicked heart;

Dictionary: Free from dirt or pollution, free from contamination or disease, pure, free from moral corruption or sinister connections, free from offensive treatment, observing the rules, ceremonially or spiritually pure.

Compassionate, kind, tender
Biblical: Compassion is a form of kindness, tenderness and sympathy, but includes something deeper; something even more profoundly powerful. To have compassion means to empathize with someone who is suffering and to feel compelled to reduce the suffering.

Dictionary: Feeling or showing sympathy and concern for others; having a sympathetic nature; having a kind, gentle, or sentimental nature.

Covetous
Biblical: An insatiable desire for worldly gain or desire to find fulfillment, meaning and purpose in things, instead of in God. The spirit of covetousness leads to and is the mother of many other sins such as coveting another man's wife or having desire for things that lead to carnality.

Dictionary: Marked by inordinate desire for wealth or possessions or for another's possessions, coveting, greedy, mercenary, moneygrubbing, rapacious.

Deceitful
Biblical: The intentional misleading or beguiling of another, in Scripture represented as a companion of many other forms of wickedness, as cursing, theft, covetousness, adultery, murder.

Dictionary: Dishonest, mendacious, untruthful or unworthy of trust or belief.

Despiteful

Biblical: The act of causing someone to accept as true or valid what is false or invalid; the act of deceiving resorting to falsehood and deception.

Dictionary: Expressing malice or hate, cruel, malevolent, malicious, mean, nasty, vicious, virulent, spiteful.

Diabolical

Biblical: Is the state of a person whose body has fallen under the control of the devil or a demon. Extremely malicious, impious, nefarious, partaking of any quality ascribed to the devil; as a diabolical temper; a diabolical scheme or action.

Dictionary: It's a characteristic of the devil, someone who concocts a devilish or diabolical plot.

Discouraged

Biblical: To extinguish the courage of; to dishearten; to depress the spirits; to deject; to deprive of confidence.; to attempt to repress or prevent to discourage an effort.

Dictionary: To deprive of courage or confidence; to hinder by disfavoring, to dissuade or attempt to dissuade from doing something.

Double

Biblical: The same as being double-minded, as in having the mind opposite or opposing views at different times. When the life is unstable the mind is unsettled and lacks solid convictions. Having a false heart; deceitful; treacherous. Being deceitful in having two parts, one openly, the other in secret.

Dictionary: Having a two-fold relation or character, consisting of two usually combined members or parts, being twice as great.

Erroneous

Biblical: A wandering or deviation from the truth; a mistake in judgment. Deviation from law, justice or right; oversight; mistake in conduct. Deviating, irregular, wandering from the right course. Misled from the truth; not comfortable to truth, erring from truth or justice.

Dictionary: Wrong or incorrect; mistaken, inaccurate; to give an erroneous impression.

Evil or Wicked

Biblical: The state of being wicked, a mental disregard for justice, righteousness, truth, honor virtue; evil in thought and life; depravity, sinfulness; criminality. Having bad qualities of a natural kind; mischievous; having qualities which tend to injury or to produce mischief. Having bad qualities of a moral kind, wicked; corrupt, perverse, as evil deeds, speaking or thoughts.

Dictionary: Morally wrong or bad, immortal; evil deeds; an evil life, harmful, detrimental; characterized or accompanied by misfortune or suffering; to be fallen on evil days, due to actual or imputed bad conduct or character; an evil reputation.

Fear of God Heart

Biblical: A joyful awareness of God's grandeur and a grateful realization that only in him do our hearts find true peace. For the believer, the fear of God is reverence of God, and the beginning of knowledge.

Dictionary: For the unbeliever, the fear of God is the fear of the judgment of God and eternal death, which is eternal separation from God.

Fixed

Biblical: The fixed heart is resolved to sing and give praise in spite of everything going on around; having determination and steadfast affection. Settled, established, firm, fast, stable.

Dictionary: Incapable of being influenced by feeling; emotionless; an immovable heart; an immovable tyrant, incapable of being moved from one's purpose, opinion, steadfast, unyielding.

Foolish and Darkened

Biblical: A foolish and darkened heart, is one which acts as though God does not exist or does not matter; willfully ignores God; an ungodly person who lacks spiritual sight; they are not intellectually deficient, but rather they are in a state of rebellion against God. Unwise, imprudent; acting without judgment or discretion in particular things. In scripture, wicked, sinful acting without regard to the divine law and glory, or to one's own eternal happiness.

Dictionary: Behavior or action that is not sensible and shows lack of good judgment, marked by a loss of composure, brainless, lunatic, senseless, simpleminded, stupid, unwise, weak-minded.

Fretting or Fretful

Biblical: Disposed to fret, ill-humored; peevish; angry; in a state of vexation; as a fretful temper. Disposition to fret and complain.

Dictionary: To be irritable or restless; being in a state of fretful despair.

Froward or Perverse

Biblical: Perverse, that is, turning from, with aversion or reluctance; not willing to yield or comply with what is required, unyielding; ungovernable, refractory, disobedient; peevish as a froward child.

Dictionary: *Froward*: Habitually disposed to disobedience and opposition; adverse to what is rational; contrary, errant, misbehaving, mischievous, naughty. *Perverse*: Turned away from what is right or good corrupt, improper, incorrect, contrary; wrongheaded, obstinate in opposing what is right.

Grieved

Biblical: Pained, afflicted, suffering sorrow.

Dictionary: To cause to suffer, being in a state of distress; to show grief over; to agonize over; in anguish, hurt, mourn, be sorrowful, suffer.

Hard or Hardened

Biblical: Made hard, or more hard or compact; made unfeeling; made obstinate; confirmed in error or vice.

Dictionary: To make hard or harder; to make callous, to confirm in disposition, feelings, or action.

Haughty

Biblical: Proud and disdainful; having a high opinion of oneself, with some contempt for others, lofty and arrogant, excessive pride or pride mingled with contempt.

Dictionary: Blatantly and disdainfully proud; having or showing an attitude of superiority and contempt for people or things perceived to be inferior. Arrogant, cavalier, chesty, high-and-mighty, huffy, lofty, pompous, assumptive, stiff-necked, uppishly or uppity.

Heart after God's Own Heart
Biblical: A man after God's own heart is not perfect; but rather is one who seeks to actively live-in obedience to God; one who responds properly when confronted with his sin. One who finds their strength in the Lord his God; one who accepts responsibility and judgment from God for his sin with humility and true repentance.

Dictionary: No Comments to match Biblical definition.

Heavy
Biblical: Heaviness in the heart of man makes it stoop, is sluggish, suffers with dullness of spirit; is weighed down with burdens and oppression.

Dictionary: Having great weight; also characterized by mass or weight; difficult to bear, in heavy sorrow or being in heavy consequences' borne down by something oppressive.

Honest and Good
Biblical: Honest, just, fair in dealing with others; free from trickiness and fraud; acting and having the disposition to always act according to justice or correct moral principles; applied to persons.

Dictionary: Good and truthful, not lying, stealing, or cheating, showing, or suggesting a good and truthful character; not hiding the truth about someone or something, not meant to deceive someone, free from fraud or deception. Genuine, real.

Idolatrous
Biblical: Pertaining to idolatry; partaking of the nature of idolatry, or of the worship of false gods; consisting in the worship of idols; as idolatrous worship. In an idolatrous manner, with excessive reverence.

Dictionary: Of or relating to idolatry which is to worship of a physical object as a god, having the character of idolatry.

Impenitent
Biblical: Not penitent; not repenting of sin; not contrite; obdurate of a hard heart. One who does not repent, a hardened sinner.

Dictionary: Not penitent, being remorseless, shameless, unashamed, unrepentant, unapologetic.

Joyful or Glad
Biblical: Full of joy; very glad, pleased, affected with pleasure or moderate joy, moderately happy.

Dictionary: Experiencing, causing, or showing joy or happiness, state of being glad, pleased, satisfied, thankful.

Meek and Lowly
Biblical: Mild of temper; soft; gentle; not easily provoked or irritated, yielding; given to forbearance under injuries. Appropriately humble, in an evangelical sense, submission to the divine will; not proud.

Dictionary: Enduring injury with patience and without resentment, submissive, not violent, or strong, down-to-earth, humble, lowly, modest, unpretentious, demure.

Melted
Biblical: Dissolved, made liquid; softened; discouraged.

Dictionary: To become subdued or crushed (as by sorrow), to become mild, tender, or gentle.

Merry
Biblical: Gay and noisy; jovial, exhilarated to laughter, causing laughter or mirth, agreeable, delightful.

Dictionary: Full of gaiety or high spirits, marked by festivity or gaiety, delightful.

Mischievous
Biblical: Harmful, hurtful, injurious, making mischief, of persons, as a mischievous manor disposition. With evil intention, or to vex or annoy.

Dictionary: Causing or tending to cause annoyance or minor harm or damage; showing a playful desire to cause trouble, intended to harm someone or someone's reputation, indulging in or instigating devilish, prankish, roguish, wicked activity.

New Heart, Stony Heart, Heart of Flesh
Biblical: Hard-hearted, cruel, pitiless; unfeeling.

Dictionary: Stony-abounding in or having the nature of stone, insensitive to pity or human feeling, manifesting no movement or reaction. Flesh- marked by consisting of, or resembling flesh, an abundant flesh.

Obstinate

Biblical: Stubborn, pertinaciously adhering to an opinion or purpose; fixed firmly in resolution, not yielding; not yielding to reason, arguments, or other means.

Dictionary: Refusing to change your behavior or your ideas, difficult to deal with, stubbornly adhering to an opinion, purpose, or course despite reason, arguments or persuasion; not easily subdued, remedied or removed.

Overcharged

Biblical: To be weighed down; loaded. Be aware of overcharge or oppress ourselves with the burdens and cares of this life, lest we fall into surfeiting (being too full of those things that are insignificant) or drunkenness with food, drink, or other influences.

Dictionary: To charge too much or too fully, to overburden, overload, encumber, saddle, or weigh down.

Perfect

Biblical: Finished; complete, consummate, not defective, having all that is requisite to its nature and kind, a perfect likeness; a perfect work; a perfect system.

Dictionary: Having no mistakes or flaws, completely correct or accurate, having all the qualities you want in that kind of person or situation, being entirely without fault or defect, corresponding to an ideal standard or abstract concept.

Proud
Biblical: Having inordinate self-esteem; possessing a high or unreasonable conceit of one's own excellence, either of body or mind. Arrogant, daring, lofty.

Dictionary: Feeling or showing pride such as having or displaying excessive self-esteem, much pleased, arrogant, haughty, overbearing, disdainful or showing scorn for inferiors; having an assumed superiority or loftiness.

Pure
Biblical: Free from moral defilement; without spot; not sullied or tarnished; incorrupt; undebased by moral turpitude; holy. Genuine, real, true, free from guilt, guiltless, innocent.

Dictionary: Unmixed with any other matter, free from dust, dirt, or taint, spotless, stainless, free from moral fault or guilt.

Single
Biblical: Separate; only one; not double, not complicated, pure, simple, incorrupt, unbiased, having clear vision of divine truth.

Dictionary: Not married, of or relating to celibacy, consisting of or having only one part, feature, or portion, consisting of only one in number, relating to, or involving only one person; frank, honest, unbroken undivided.

Soft
Biblical: A soft heart learns that true strength is in maintaining a good relationship with Jesus Christ, while being able to maintain relational success with others. A heart that shows love and compassion to others.

Dictionary: Not bright or glaring, quiet in pitch or volume, demanding little work or effort, easy, not harsh, or onerous in character, tending to take a soft line. Mildness, low-key, unassuming, unduly susceptible to influence, lacking firmness or strength of character, lacking robust strength, stamina, or endurance, weak or deficient mentally.

Sorrowful

Biblical: Penitence is the state of being sorrowful over one's flaws or actions. One who has deep remorse that motivates a change in behavior and does everything possible to make amends. Penitence involves humility, regret, and sorrow is the avenue God has provided for us to receive His forgiveness.

Dictionary: Full of or marked by sorrow, expressive of or inducing sorrow, aching, agonized, anguished, bitter, grieving, heartbroken, mournful, regretful, sorry, weeping, woeful.

Steadfast

Biblical: Sad; grieving for the loss of some good, or on account of some expected evil, deeply serious, depressed, dejected. Producing sorrow, mournful.

Dictionary: Firmly fixed in place, immovable, not subject to change, firm in belief, determination, or adherence, loyal. Constant, dedicated, devoted, faithful, staunch, steady, true.

Stubborn

Biblical: Unreasonably obstinate; inflexibly fixed in opinion; not to be moved or persuaded by reasons, inflexible; as a stubborn son; a stubborn mind or soul, persisting, stubborn to justice. Resisting command.

Dictionary: Refusing to change your ideas or to stop doing something, difficult to deal with, unreasonably or perversely unyielding, strong stubborn nature, difficult to handle, manage.

Subtle (Subtil)

Biblical: Sly in design; artful; cunning; insinuating; planned by art; deceitful, treacherous. Thin not dense or gross, refined, fine; acute as a subtil argument.

Dictionary: Hard to notice or see, not obvious, clever, and indirect, not showing your real purpose, having or showing skill at recognizing and understanding things that are not obvious, perceptive. Delicate, elusive.

Tender

Biblical: Having great sensibility; susceptible of impressions or influence, susceptible of the softer passions of love, pity, or kindness.

Dictionary: Very loving and gentle, showing affection and love for someone or something, expressing the softer emotions fond, loving, considerate. Sensitive to injury or insult, physically weak, not able to endure hardship, immature, young. Appropriate or conducive to a delicate or sensitive constitution or character, gentle, mild.

Tranquil

Biblical: Undisturbed, peaceful; not agitated, calm, quietness.

Dictionary: Quiet and peaceful, free from agitation of mind or spirit, free from disturbance or turmoil, steady, stable.

Trembling

Biblical: Shaking as with fear, cold or weakness, quaking, shivering.

Dictionary: To shake involuntarily to shiver, to be affected with great fear or anxiety, to quiver, to quiver shiver or shutter. a fit or spell of involuntary shaking or quivering.

Troubled
Biblical: Disturbed, agitated, afflicted; annoyed. The primary sense is to turn or to stir, to whirl about, the sense of agitation, disturbance. To agitate, to put in a confused motion.

Dictionary: Concerned, worried, exhibiting emotional or behavioral problems, characterized by or indicative of trouble

True
Biblical: Conformable to fact; being in accordance with the actual state of things; as a true relation or narration; a true history. A declaration is true when it states the facts. Genuine, pure; real, not counterfeit, adulterated or false. Honest not fraudulent.

Dictionary: Bring in accordance with the actual state of affairs, conformable to an essential reality, fully realized or fulfilled, ideal essential, consistent. Being that which is the case rather than what is manifest or assumed. Ideal, essential, consistent, and true to character, steadfast, loyal, honest, just, truthful.

Turned Away
Biblical: To turn away from God is to divert your worship, devotion, and loyalty from the Lord and to bestow them to another thing or person. It could be your job, relationship, or other idols as they get carried away by other doctrines that appeal to their sinful nature.

Dictionary: To refuse admittance or acceptance too, to send away, reject, dismiss, repel, deflect. To turn back.

Uncircumcised
Biblical: Not circumcised.

Dictionary: Not circumcised, spiritually impure, as in a heathen.

Unsearchable
Biblical: That cannot be searched or explored, inscrutable, hidden, mysterious. The quality or state of being unsearchable, or beyond the power of man to explore.

Dictionary: Not capable of being searched or explored, inscrutable.

Upright
Biblical: Honest; just, not deviating from correct moral principles, as an upright man. Integrity in principle or practice; conformity to rectitude and justice in social dealings.

Dictionary: Erect in carriage or posture, having the main axis or a main part perpendicular, marked by strong moral rectitude. Decent, ethical, good, honest, just, moral, righteous, honorable.

Whorish
Biblical: Lewd, unchaste; addicted to unlawful sexual pleasures; incontinent. The practice of lewdness.

Dictionary: Of or befitting a whore, a promiscuous or immoral man or woman, an unscrupulous person, to pursue a faithless, unworthy, or idolatrous desire, to corrupt by lewd intercourse.

Willing
Biblical: Free to do or grant; having the mind inclined; disposed, not averse, ready, prompt, having a free heart, with free will; without reluctance, cheerfully, by one's own choice.

Dictionary: Inclined or favorably disposed in mind, ready, willing, and eager to help; prompt to act or respond, of or relating to the will or power of choosing, acceptance by choice or without reluctance. Voluntary, intentional, deliberate, implies freedom and spontaneity of choice or action without external compulsion.

Wise

Biblical: Properly, having knowledge; having the power of discerning and judging correctly or of discriminating between what is true and what is false' between what is fit and proper, and what is improper. Discrete and judicious in the use or applications of knowledge; choosing laudable ends, and the best means to accomplish them.

Dictionary: Characterized by wisdom, marked by deep understanding, keen discernment, and a capacity for sound judgment; exercising or showing sound judgment, prudent, knowing, being knowledgeable, to give instruction or information to.

Dictionary source: Merriam-Webster

www.ingramcontent.com/pod-product-compliance
Lightning Source LLC
Chambersburg PA
CBHW052112030426
42335CB00025B/2952